theatre & the visual

Theatre&
Series Editors: Jen Harvie and Dan Rebellato

Theatre& Series
Series Standing Order: ISBN 978–0–333–230–20327–3

You can receive future titles in this series as they are published by placing a standing order. Please contact your bookseller or, in case of difficulty, write to us at the address below with your name and address, the title of the series and the ISBN quoted above.

Customer Services Department, Macmillan Distribution Ltd
Houndmills, Basingstoke, Hampshire RG21 6XS, England

theatre & the visual

Dominic Johnson

palgrave
macmillan

First published 2012 by
PALGRAVE MACMILLAN

Palgrave Macmillan in the UK is an imprint of Macmillan Publishers Limited, registered in England, company number 785998, of Houndmills, Basingstoke, Hampshire RG21 6XS.

Palgrave Macmillan in the US is a division of St Martin's Press LLC, 175 Fifth Avenue, New York, NY 10010.

Palgrave Macmillan is the global academic imprint of the above companies and has companies and representatives throughout the world.

Palgrave® and Macmillan® are registered trademarks in the United States, the United Kingdom, Europe and other countries

ISBN: 978–0–230–24662–1 paperback

This book is printed on paper suitable for recycling and made from fully managed and sustained forest sources. Logging, pulping and manufacturing processes are expected to conform to the environmental regulations of the country of origin.

A catalogue record for this book is available from the British Library.

A catalog record for this book is available from the Library of Congress.

10 9 8 7 6 5 4 3 2 1
21 20 19 18 17 16 15 14 13 12

Printed in China

contents

series editors' preface

The theatre is everywhere, from entertainment districts to the fringes, from the rituals of government to the ceremony of the courtroom, from the spectacle of the sporting arena to the theatres of war. Across these many forms stretches a theatrical continuum through which cultures both assert and question themselves.

Theatre has been around for thousands of years, and the ways we study it have changed decisively. It's no longer enough to limit our attention to the canon of Western dramatic literature. Theatre has taken its place within a broad spectrum of performance, connecting it with the wider forces of ritual and revolt that thread through so many spheres of human culture. In turn, this has helped make connections across disciplines; over the past fifty years, theatre and performance have been deployed as key metaphors and practices with which to rethink gender, economics, war, language, the fine arts, culture and one's sense of self.

Theatre & is a long series of short books which hopes to capture the restless <u>interdisciplinary</u> energy of theatre and performance. Each book explores connections between theatre and some aspect of the wider world, asking how the theatre might <u>illuminate the world</u> and how the world might illuminate the theatre. Each book is written by a leading theatre <u>scholar</u> and represents the cutting edge of critical thinking in the <u>discipline</u>.

We have been mindful, however, that the philosophical and theoretical complexity of much contemporary academic writing can act as a barrier to a wider readership. A key aim for these books is that they should all be readable in one sitting by anyone with a curiosity about the subject. The books are <u>challenging</u>, pugnacious, visionary sometimes and, above all, clear. We hope you enjoy them.

Jen Harvie and Dan Rebellato

foreword: permission to play

I find the people I want to photograph everywhere. They are the people I find irresistible. I may be walking down the street or sitting on a bus, in a club or in a café when I see her. She has caught my eye. I look. Giving myself permission to look. I may even find myself staring, lost in the fantasy of her face. She has a presence that captures me completely. I want her. I want to see. I want to know. I want to have, if only for an instant. This is my most vulnerable moment. If my gaze is returned I try to smile and not let the embarrassment of being caught looking, caught with my desire exposed for all to see, jeopardize what could be the start of a beautiful relationship. If I'm feeling in the slightest bit dashing I will walk over and introduce myself by way of my fascination with her face and form. Briefly stating my purpose I suggest we meet at a later date to discuss my proposition in depth. If this initial seduction is successful (which it usually is when I feel dashing), we move on to the negotiation stage, either a continuation of the seduction or simply a stating of boundaries, hopes and fears that eventually leads to the photographic moment. Not the 'decisive moment' so treasured by Henri Cartier-Bresson, but a series of moments, from the instant my eye lands upon her body to the moment yours does.

Flattery goes a very long way with me and is what brings these words and reflections, memories and images, from my past and present from me to you. I'm looking at a catalogue for *The Eighth Square: Gender, Life and Desire in the Arts since 1960* from the Museum Ludwig in Cologne. This was the first queer exhibition in a major European museum and I was thrilled to be part of it. The image they used for the cover of the catalogue is by Wolfgang Tillmans: a close-up of a man's naked arse, cock and balls, taken from the perspective of someone lying on the ground looking up. It promises much but actually delivers nothing except a hairy arse, as the title covers the family jewels. It reminds me how we all like to look at things we aren't supposed to. It reminds me of the time I was four years old and under the skirt of a very fat woman. I'm not sure how I got there but everyone knew exactly where I was when I shouted, 'The fat lady isn't wearing any underpants!' That was not the first time I got into trouble for looking.

A few years back one of my young multi-national, multi-lingual cousins put a hand on my arm and sombrely asked, 'What *are* you?' As one of the things that I *am* is a 'herm' (hermaphrodite/hermaphro*dyke*/intersex/intergender *and* trans), I suspected this question was another way of asking whether I was a boy or a girl. But I didn't want to assume, so I responded with a question: 'I'm not sure. What are *you*?' With big brown eyes open wide, the response was, 'I am a *children*.' Which allowed me to give the appropriate answer, that I was an adult.

As a young child I was constantly told off for staring at people. Staring but not smiling, looking but not laughing. For a person assigned female at birth this was definitely not 'on'. But I liked to look and still do. As an adult I've reluctantly adapted to social conventions and try to avoid making people uncomfortable just because I find them enticing, exciting or enchanting.

Mika Alexis Volcano is a living, breathing child that I get to keep, and who has become an avatar of sorts. Not only a *super*human but a creature that has cultural permission to behave in ways that I, sadly, do not. We spend a couple hours every week on buses travelling to where Mika's other parent works to breastfeed. On the way there it's impossible not to notice how most kids are ignored and kept captive in their high-tech Swedish prams. Mika prefers to be in my arms, jumping up and down and making sure that all eyes are directed towards us. S/he also likes to look, especially at people, and stares them down until they have no choice but to look back and respond. A few people have confessed to being unnerved by the intensity of Mika's gaze, and I love it. This is one kid who will never be punished for looking.

I have a *career* of sorts, which I prefer to think of as a kind of evangelical calling. I'm a photographer who makes (rather than takes) images from subjects who get to speak.

I know that most people really want and need to be seen: as they see themselves and as they wish others would see them. I know how to do that. I do it for myself. I have to.

In *La Pointe à l'oeil*, the art historian Jean Clair wrote, 'Vision is not only a passive, feminine receptacle where the real gets photographed, but it is also a phalloid organ able to unfold and erect itself out of its cavity and point towards the visible. The gaze is the erection of the eye' (Paris: Cahier du Musée National d'Art Moderne, 1983). There are a few people in my life who allow me to get my (metaphorical) erection out and stroke it as I look at them. I know that sounds obscene, and if you think I said it just to get your attention you're probably right. Here's the thing. Looking, *really* looking, turns me on. Always has, always will. Not just the act but the action.

I occasionally share my very small flat in London with a person I find utterly delectable. His work is part of this book. Ron Athey is famous for a lot of things, and one of them is being looked at. (He has also been photographed, a lot, but strangely not by me.) If he were a taste, as in one of the five basic tastes, he would be *umami*, which is pretty much untranslatable from Japanese, but means something like 'mouth-watering', just like the visceral pleasure I get when we are together. While I have no interest in getting 'genital' with Ron (and I'm sure the feeling is mutual), I can't deny that the pleasure I get looking at his body, both in and out of clothes, is a super-sexual experience. And while there are five books full of people who turn me on in one way or another, from *Love Bites* to *Femmes of Power*, the difference with my roomie is that I don't have to hide my hard-on with him. We embody the very definition of a mutually beneficial relationship.

Most of the photographs I make with people use the world as our stage, as a backdrop for the performance of our selves. The dykes in my first book, *Love Bites*, were all regulars at Chain Reaction, a lesbian sex and performance club launched at the Market Tavern in Vauxhall in the late 1980s. Our motto was 'Permission to Play'. Since the club was one of the only 'safe spaces' available to us back then I took very few photos inside. Instead we created some rockstar sex spectaculars in pre-Clause 28 London, from public parks to Soho rooftops. Every photo shoot was a 'happening' with active voyeurs and exhibitionists. We performed for ourselves and each other and the sheer power of being 'bad' just for the sake of pleasure. *Love Bites* was published in 1991 and although mainstream bookstores sold it, wrapped in an impenetrable see-through cover, the lesbian/gay bookstores at the time, Gay's The Word, Silvermoon and Sisterwrite, refused to stock it due to its politically incorrect SM content. It was also briefly seized by Customs in the USA. And it sold a lot of copies.

Allow me to get Californian on you and speak astrologically for a moment. I have an imbalance. I'm a veritable stellium of fire. A Leo with Leo Rising and Uranus riding my Sun like a hot poker up the arse. Truly. And that's just my 12th House. Add to this Mercury, Mars, Pluto and Venus, all in Leo in the 1st House, and maybe you can see why I might have been considered 'too much' growing up. In case you didn't know, Leo is ruled by the Sun, likes to be the centre of attention and is the ruling planet of both children and the theatre. Barack Obama, Bill Clinton and Osama bin Laden are/were all Leos, but not fortunate enough to have been born on *my* birthday. Aldous Huxley, Helen Mirren, Kevin Spacey, Mojisola Adebayo, Sandra Bullock, Mick Jagger, Carl Jung, George Bernard Shaw, Stanley Kubrick and Jason Robards were. Egotism can be a problem, but most of us don't want to be the only celestial bodies in the sky. We want our heat to warm other bodies. We want our light to bounce around and illuminate those dark dirty corners where secrets are stuffed.

Performers are all Leos underneath the skin. Theatre was invented so that adults could show off and be applauded for it.

Del LaGrace Volcano

theatre & the visual

Introduction

Experiences in the theatre are often characterised by memorable situations of looking. Theatre history abounds with plays about the pleasures and pains of picturing a world, and the social dramas of looking and being seen. What we see, in the theatre and elsewhere, is conditioned by the act of looking, where we look from, how we look, and why we look away. If we look askew at the theatre and its events, with a particular focus on visual experience, intriguing questions emerge, which this book investigates. How does the theatrical image – what is revealed or concealed in performance – produce effects? If we are accustomed to looking at bodies, what happens when they look back at us, in affectively charged theatrical encounters? How do images produce pleasure? What happens when an image inflicts pain, or hurts the viewer? Why are performed images seemingly more prone to shocking or upsetting audiences than the spoken word? These and other questions prompt an analysis of the politics of vision, and suggest that theatre is a promising venue in which to train our gaze.

I argue that the act of looking in the theatre must be accounted for through an understanding of theatricality and visuality, two terms that highlight the contingency of making meaning in the theatre. This emphasis on the volatility of visual experience allows me to explore the intriguing political work facilitated by looking, searching, staring, and averting our gaze. A key argument of *Theatre & the Visual* is that our persistent fascination with looking and being seen – and the trouble these activities cause us – is significant to cultural engagement in general, but is pronounced in our responses to theatrical representation.

In Part One, I suggest that what historical subjects have seen in the theatre has been affected not simply by the events, acts, and identities produced or described by dramatists. Historical conditions of production enabled new ways of seeing and novel ways of making meaning in the theatre. I argue that vision itself has a history, which consists of dominant models for looking, as well as 'visual subcultures'. The event of visual experience tends to remind viewers that the ways we look can be the basis for political engagement with the theatre and with the world. These arguments set the scene, in Part Two, for a study of the production of wordless spectacles, or events that privilege imagery over spoken texts, to suggest how audiences experience different affects when looking in the theatre. I will suggest that performance artists, especially, have found provocative ways to test

2

the relations between theatre and the visual. Performances by Franko B, Annie Sprinkle, and Ron Athey, for example, forcefully challenge the primacy of the pre-written text, in favour of visually powerful live works. By troubling established hierarchies between the visual and the verbal in the theatre, they further muddy the ditch between word and image. Part Three balances this emphasis on the troubled pleasures that theatre offers, arguing that experimental performance explores the pain of looking as a means of staging the politics of the visual. Throughout, I emphasise situations of extremity as instances where the problems of vision are thrown into particular relief. A short epilogue asks how shocked perception is a litmus test for the historicity of any understanding of the relation between theatre and the visual, or between theatricality and visuality.

Hide and seek

'The visual' seems to emerge – inevitably – wherever one looks in the theatre. This methodological problem is compounded by the central difficulty of separating out seeing from hearing in performance. Nevertheless, one of the key assumptions of this book is that the privileged status of written texts – and the attendant experience of listening to words – functions at the expense of a theory of visual perception in the theatre. The apparent marginality of visual perception in the theatre is suggested by the English word for theatregoers – 'audience' – whose root is the Latin *audire*, meaning 'to hear'. Yet the theatrical endeavour is rarely (if ever) undertaken solely as an auditory experience.

Attending the theatre, an audience undergoes a jostling of sensory experiences; this tests the supposedly primary function of receiving and deciphering a recited text. The theatre always troubles the relation between the visual and the textual, specifically by asking how the written word – the published script, programme, and other textual remnants of live performance – is usually privileged to the detriment of the sensory experience of visiting and engaging with a theatrical production. Artists and theorists alike have noticed this troublesome potential in the theatre. In his essay 'Writing Silence' (2010), the British director and performer Neil Bartlett states that in (primarily visual) forms such as mime, pantomime, puppetry, dance, physical theatre, or performance art – but also, crucially, in 'straight' theatre – 'what we feel and see is happening to those people up there under the lights is just as important as what we can hear them saying' (p. 5).

The theatrical experience depends on complex relationships between vision and other forms of sensory perception. Upon the scaffold of textual production and delivery, a team of creators often builds a further system of visual signs, including scenography, dramaturgy, set and lighting design, costume and make-up, marketing content, and the blocking or choreography of performers' movements. Visual signs conspire to produce meaning for the viewer, as they emphasise or undermine the words that may be spoken by performers. Other types of experience, including the material, temporal, social, and environmental conditions of theatrical production and reception, supplement these stimuli.

4

Therefore, in even the most traditional theatre productions, the text wrestles – for primacy, or equanimity – with other modes of representation and perception, including what is shown or concealed in the visual world of the theatre.

However, problems arise if we over-determine the visual as the primary experience in the theatre, over and above the perception of words and other non-visual signs. I encourage a more nuanced understanding of the relation between the verbal and the visual, as different models of representation, because the attempt to privilege one system over the other is determined by the political, cultural, and social assumptions of any particular moment. As W. J. T. Mitchell argues in *Iconology* (1987), the relation between image and text is an ideological one: 'a struggle that carries the fundamental contradictions of [a] culture into the heart of theoretical discourse itself' (p. 44). Rather than simply analyse, organise, or fix the hierarchy between image and text, then, we must historicise the relationship, and examine the wider cultural implications of one order of representation feigning primacy over another (pp. 42–44).

Images in traditional theatre are often crafted from stage directions, or directorial interpretations of play texts. These images can give rise to vivid experiences that leave their mark upon audiences. In this book I analyse a series of instances where the visual is emphasised as an important aspect of the theatrical experience. Later examples include performance art events, which some readers might disregard as unrepresentative of general experiences of theatre's exploitation of the visual. Experimental practices may depart from the conventions of traditional theatre, but performance art, dance, puppetry, mime, and other frequently visual forms are nevertheless conditioned by theatrical modes of production and reception. A key theme of this book is that what we see in the theatre is an effect of what is concealed. Similarly, it could be said that in any performance, what we see often depends upon relationships to theatre that are evoked but not explicitly staged or performed.

The visible elements of a theatrical production are therefore ghosted by ideas, identities, and histories that may evade full representation. This is not to say that theatre's inability, reluctance, or refusal to show certain things is a weakness. On the contrary, theatre often plays powerfully with the anomalous visual effects of hiding and revealing. The conclusion to Henrik Ibsen's realist drama *Ghosts* (1881), for example, presents the disease-wracked remnants of Osvald Alving seated in an armchair, facing the audience. In Ibsen's stage directions, a sun rises to frame the aftermaths of Osvald's inheritance of his father's syphilis. Without moving, and blind to the distant glow of a sunrise, Osvald demands, 'Mother, give me the sun.' The statement creates a powerful, enigmatic verbal image, evoking both the gravity of parental inheritances – moral, psychological, physiological – and a lexical obscurity that indexes Osvald's madness. 'Osvald seems to shrink in the chair', reads Ibsen's stage direction; 'all his muscles go slack, his face is without expression, and his eyes stare vacantly.' The image suggests youthful vivacity being sapped from Osvald's body, and gives way to a visual event that exceeds the play's pale horror, namely the grim spectacle of Mrs Alving rifling hurriedly through her son's pockets, searching for poison capsules in order to euthanise him. Standing back, hands twisted in her hair, Mrs Alving looks on with dread and terror as her son slumps against a vivid blaze of light. As he utters his final, enigmatic words, 'The sun ... the sun', the curtains fall upon the disastrous scene (pp. 101–2).

Ibsen's horrific denouement gestures to the cultural impact of showing social ills, and dramatises taste and decorum as meagre strategies for concealing them (signified in Pastor Manders' earlier attempts to overwrite the family's historical indiscretions, by preserving their secret status). Family histories are made manifest in the catastrophic image of the son's madness and impending death. When the audience watches Osvald's decline into syphilitic incapacity, we bear witness to the invisible weight of a family's hidden histories: its tales of debauchery, adultery, incest, and duplicity that might otherwise evade visibility. Ibsen's play was a landmark text in modern drama, and established a vogue for realist theatrical representation in the twentieth century. In its final moments, *Ghosts* privileges the audience as a group of individuals caught up in the act of looking, as the narrative of concealment and exposure coheres into a visually charged, scandalous image.

Playwrights have toyed persistently with the drama of hiding and revealing, and the peculiar pleasures this tactic invokes. While the tactic of hiding and revealing has been central to theatrical representation at least since classical Greek drama, its significance in terms of sexuality has become very clear since the development of modern theatrical realism. Tennessee Williams' *Cat on a Hot Tin Roof* (1955) is a classic play that also relishes the visual possibilities that emerge from dramatising the attempt to keep secrets hidden. In two initial pages of notes to the designer, Williams painstakingly describes the room in which the play's action takes place, creating a visual tension between important architectural signifiers and the secret lives that reside within the scenery. The setting is a bed-sitting-room in a plantation house in the Mississippi Delta, decorated with ornate balustrades and Orientalist kitsch, which reflects the tastes of the room's previous occupants, 'a pair of old bachelors who shared this room all their lives together' (p. 5). Some of the notes describe things the audience is instructed to see, such as a double bed, suggesting the forbidden romances the room has housed. This suggested history contrasts with the relationship between the main characters, Brick and Maggie, whose overwrought but sexless marriage drives much of the play's dramatic conflict.

The playwright's notes also describe elements that cannot be seen directly: 'the room must evoke some ghosts; it is gently and poetically haunted by a relationship that must have involved a tenderness which was uncommon', a haunting that Williams compares quixotically to 'a quality of tender light on weathered wood' (p. 5). If Williams deploys games of hide and seek towards a politically invested strategy of show and tell, he does so in order to make his audience 'see' what is hidden, namely Brick's fraught concealment of his apparent homosexuality. Like *Ghosts*, the play's dramatic effect depends on the intense emotional charge of the phenomenon of the open secret.

Maggie is a harridan. Her husband Brick is conservative and uptight, and has descended into alcoholism since the death of Skipper, a friend he was unable to address as a lover. 'When something is festering in your memory or your imagination,' Maggie tells him after the first mention of Skipper, 'laws of silence don't work, it's just like shutting a door and locking it on a house on fire in hope of forgetting that the house is burning' (p. 18). Maggie gestures to the 'ghosts' that Brick cannot allow to be made manifest, and the seemingly paradoxical theatrical effects of ostentatious acts of hiding. The audience hears more than it sees, but a secret image looms large upon the scene. 'Silence about a thing just magnifies it,' Maggie says, highlighting the way that events the audience doesn't quite see are nevertheless subject to signification in the dark recesses of the play (p. 18).

These two canonical plays suggest there are political dimensions to what is shown and what remains hidden in the theatre. As Mrs Alving states, 'it's not only the things that we've inherited from our fathers and mothers that live on in us, but all sorts of old dead ideas and old dead beliefs' – the 'ghosts' that wreak havoc with the doomed characters when secrets are disclosed – 'outed' – in the play (p. 61). In *Cat on a Hot Tin Roof*, however, what we never see raises political questions, by gesturing enigmatically to conditions of experience that resist full representation: covertly, yet with powerful dramatic effects. Specifically, while the spectacle of homosexuality is never seen in *Cat on a Hot Tin*

Roof, the play dramatises the space of the closet – and the differing yet related ways in which the character (Brick) and the playwright (Williams) inhabited it.

Seeing homosexuality in mid-century drama might have invited the censor's red pen, so sexuality – like the 'closet' – is shown to the extent it remains hidden (secret, that is, but showily so). Similarly, although *Ghosts* appalled early critics, we never quite see the 'degenerate' practices or the most 'dissolute' characters that fuel the play's ignominious sequence of events. Ibsen and Williams highlight the particularity of an audience's responses to performance. They gesture to the contingency of vision as a crucial influence upon the meanings produced by reception. Our practices of seeing are thoroughly and irremediably conditioned by the places from which we look, and by our constitution as historical subjects.

The contingency of vision

As these preliminary examples suggest, *Theatre & the Visual* considers the political implications of the visual in the scopic regime governing theatrical culture. 'Scopic regime' is a term used by Martin Jay and other theorists to discuss the historical breaks between successive ways of looking. Scopic regimes govern what we look at, how we look, and why. The notion of a 'regime' of the 'scopic' – the latter from *skopein*, a Greek word meaning 'to look at' or 'to view' – signals the understanding that vision is governed by political logics. The term suggests that the ways we view the world are never neutral, but can be examined according to the ideologies that underpin the specific place and time from which we look. The same ideologies also affect how others see us, on or off the stage. I take a parallax view of the theatre by privileging visual experience, towards an interdisciplinary theory of 'visuality'. A 'parallax' approach pulls the point of view into oblique angles, throwing the place one looks from into unfamiliar perspectives.

Visuality is a crucial concept for examining the contingent relations between theatre and the visual. While historical contingencies affect what and how we see, vision also has some basic physiological aspects. Very briefly, the trans-historical phenomena of human optics include the problems posed by the human eye's ability to process only 1 per cent of the light waves that it apprehends; a blind spot in the visual field, where the optic nerve meets the retina, but which the brain patches over for the sake of continuity of vision; saccadic vision, or the inability of the human eye to pan across a scene, which it overcomes by moving swiftly from one fixated point to another; three-dimensional perception, which muddles the visual information provided by each of two eyes; and the vergence system, where the brain fuses short- and long-range focus into one coherent visual experience. Jay usefully summarises the biological aspects of vision in *Downcast Eyes* (1993, pp. 7–8).

By contrasting the biology of optics with the social practices of visuality, visual studies scholars show that vision relies on a much larger set of historical and cultural factors than can be explained by physiology. For Hal Foster, in his preface to *Vision and Visuality* (1988), the difference between optics and a social theory of visuality suggests 'a difference within the visual – between the mechanism of sight and its historical techniques' (p. ix). A theory of vision in the theatre and elsewhere, therefore, must distinguish between the idea of vision as a simple biological activity and the more complex question of how visuality has been constructed historically as a politically invested act.

Neologisms such as 'scopic regime' and 'visuality' sometimes cause irritation, not least because they seem to suggest that a problem can be solved through an act of linguistic inventiveness. The 'problem' for visuality is the curious question of how images work, and the popular assumption that visual perception is a politically neutral, merely biological element of human experience. Critical theory suggests that when a concept presents itself as neutral, natural, or biological there are hidden political issues that need to be addressed. Therefore, as a *cultural* activity that risks being reduced to the status of a physiological operation, visual experience necessitates new words and nuanced theories. Drawn from visual studies (a development of art history), 'visuality' suggests the 'historicity' or historically situated aspects of looking at objects, bodies, or events. In the remainder of this introduction, I set out some general, preliminary ideas about the ways images seem to work, including the problem of extremity, the contingency of vision, and the necessarily interdisciplinary condition of focusing one's attention on theatre and the visual.

Visual extremities

In recent years, playwrights have often explored the politics of theatre by foregrounding the pleasures and pains of challenging visual experiences. In *The Author* (The Royal Court Theatre Upstairs, London, 2009), the British theatre artist Tim Crouch summarises recent attempts to jolt audiences into acknowledging the power of visual experience in the theatre. Playing a version of himself in *The Author*, the performance artist Adrian Howells says, 'I've seen everything imaginable here' (p. 46). The line is delivered in an upbeat tone that registers his character Adrian's unflappable enthusiasm for the theatre and the spectacles it stages. Sitting among the audience in the small Royal Court Theatre Upstairs, Adrian gives a sensational overview of the visual highs and lows of recent British theatre:

> I've seen bum sex and rimming and cock sucking and wankings and rapings and stabbings and shootings and bombings. Bombings and bummings! I've seen someone shit on a table! I've seen a man have his eyes sucked out. I've seen so many blindings! And stonings. [...] I've seen a dead baby get eaten! That was great! (pp. 46–47)

The character narrates forty years of British theatrical notoriety, from a scene where we see a 'baby stoned to death' in a pram in Edward Bond's *Saved* (Royal Court Theatre, London, 1965) to the 'wankings' and 'stabbings' of Anthony Neilson's *Penetrator* (Traverse Theatre, Edinburgh, 1994); cannibalism, 'blindings', 'bombings' and 'rapings' in Sarah Kane's *Blasted* (Royal Court Theatre Upstairs, London, 1995);

and 'rimming' and 'bum sex' in Mark Ravenhill's *Shopping and Fucking* (Royal Court Theatre Upstairs/Ambassadors Theatre, London, 1996). Theatrical experimentation is caricatured as so many visual extremities – sexual, abusive, or violent excesses at a limit of culture – that perhaps characterise 'new writing' in the late twentieth century. While Crouch's play comments on the centrality of looking in the history of the theatre, *The Author* is a peculiarly non-visual event in itself. Yet straying from the powers of the visual does not interrupt his play's ability to surprise its audiences.

Critiquing the dominant culture of realist drama from Ibsen to Williams, contemporary theatre artists have urged for more and more nuanced explorations of the performed image. Their works have staged the capacities of theatrical images to educate, gratify, move, offend, and hurt the spectator. Adrian's monologue in *The Author* troubles this account, by suggesting the volatile pleasures initiated by visual excess. He summarises the thrill of watching violent actions as 'great', and this ironic revelry in theatrical depravity has provocative implications later in the play, when the audience is invited to cast judgment on Tim (played by Crouch himself) after he confesses to consuming child pornography in a setting that amplifies how repugnant his actions are. It is the beginning of an arduous, ethically uncomfortable ending, not least because we listen to Tim's detailed revelation in pitch darkness, and a grim flood of verbal images fills the scene. The tendency to see violent acts in the contemporary theatre is signalled yet denied here, condensing the strategies playwrights have used to reveal and

14

hide difficult subject matter – those in the plays he gestures to explicitly, and those in relatively distant landmarks such as *Ghosts* or *Cat on a Hot Tin Roof*. Relayed in words rather than frank visual content, Crouch's verbal images still graze the mind's eye. *The Author* demonstrates how contemporary theatre has self-consciously investigated the historical and political roles that visual experience plays for critical audiences.

In *The Author*, the audience's difficulty emerges from our conspicuous failure to separate aural from visual experience. I argue that 'difficult' performances often demonstrate the complexity of visual experience, and prioritise the historical contingency of theatrical reading practices. In many ways, then, this book approaches the relation between theatre and the visual through the specific difficulty of 'visual extremity'. Throughout I ask how, precisely, performed images produce meaning for audiences in specific times and places. Instances of extremity suggest that it is at the limits of media, cultures, and histories that relevant questions are asked anew.

How do images work?

Whether we consider works of art, performances, or mass-cultural depictions – or other, particularly anomalous images, such as the visual content of dreams – images can seem full or empty, lucid or baffling, tightly composed or poorly conceived. Certain images might appear to resist legibility altogether, hence the confusion and frustration that abstract art or contemporary dance can induce in

audiences. Moreover, all images have the capacity to produce meanings that emerge from unexpected sources, against
the wishes of the producer, which explains the apparently
accidental offence caused by some images. These possibilities are seemingly accentuated when images are produced
and received in the space of live performance. In live art
and performance art, especially, such images are relieved
of the burden of narrative, or other conventional textual
frameworks. How do we attend to such images, which seem
to produce meanings much more unpredictably than a written text might?

The theorist Roland Barthes was one of the most influ-
ential thinkers to analyse the system through which visual
compositions make (or confound) meaning. In 'The Rhetoric
of the Image' (1964), he showed that the image is a rudimen-
tary system in comparison to written or verbal language,
yet still relies on sophisticated techniques to produce meaning for viewers. 'How does meaning get into the image?'
Barthes asked. 'Where does it end? And if it ends, what is
there beyond?' (p. 32). Barthes' questions are trained upon
utilitarian images, but relate closely to the problem of how
performed images might enable or inhibit the production of
meaning. By analysing a generic advertisement for an Italian
brand of groceries, Barthes demonstrated that specific meanings can be written into images, but that the image also has a
'beyond', where the potential for meaning is less confidently
determined by the producer. It is this beyond that performance often revels in, unleashing the power of images to confound, excite, and unsettle audiences.

To return to Ibsen's *Ghosts*, the catastrophic finale might act as a symbol: of the legacies of slackened moral principles, or of the centrality of violence for the historical production of dramatic narrative. Moreover, the spectacle of Osvald's decline into madness and impending death serves as a trigger for the performative function of theatrical images. Images in the theatre *do* more than they *mean*. Performances act upon audiences, spaces, histories, and cultures, and call into question our assumptions about the world. For example, by producing affective responses – anxiety, disturbance, concern, fear, horror – Osvald's ravings remind us that the theatre has often trained its gaze upon the potential for images to unsettle its audiences. The performed image of his death reminds us vicariously of the thrill of being a living body that contends with the lives of others, in seemingly volatile social situations that ask us to negotiate a range of difficult impulses and emotions.

Barthes showed that audiences are canny readers of images. Adverts are a useful type of image to study, because they rely on complex techniques to convey 'intentional signification' to massive audiences – more so, perhaps, than the theatre does. Barthes noted that advertising produces images that are generally 'frank' and 'emphatic' about their intentions. Unlike visual art, theatre, and performance, adverts work by securing an optimum reading in order to produce a desired effect (suggestible consumers of the image are induced to buy the product it advertises). They do so through three modes of signification, which combine to form the system or rhetoric of the image.

The most straightforward mode is the written or 'linguistic' message of the image, which includes the brand, labels, captions, and carefully worded statements it might contain. Art and non-literary performance may be predominantly visual systems, but they are hardly devoid of linguistic messages, from the words contained in paintings (for example, the pop art of Roy Lichtenstein, in which a cartoon explosion screams the painted word 'Blam!') to the words that might accompany wordless spectacles, as titles, programme notes, or marketing materials.

The second mode, the coded or 'denoted' message, relies on a higher level of complexity. This is the slightly hazier system through which specific objects or textures seem to evoke an idea that is symbolised, but not explicitly referenced, and relies on culturally contingent knowledge. In Barthes' advert, for example, shiny ripe fruits and vegetables sit alongside branded produce, and the iconic suggestions of freshness, nature, health, and plenty pass from the former to the latter. Theatre revels in the production of these denoted messages. An example in *Ghosts* is the literal relation between Osvald's body and the disastrous histories that 'ghost' his doomed family. The denoted message is more complex than the linguistic message, because it is 'discontinuous', metaphorical, and open to misfiring. Nevertheless, it works by creating literal relationships between two signs.

The third mode of signification is the 'connoted' image, where the various parts of the system come together to create a higher level of complexity that depends on the symbolic powers of colour, shape, scale, depth, and other visual factors. In *Cat on a Hot Tin Roof*, Williams' imagined set can be understood as a connoted image: he writes, 'the walls below the ceiling should dissolve mysteriously into air; the set should be roofed by the sky; the stars and moon suggested by traces of milky pallor, as if they were observed through a telescope lens out of focus' (p. 6). A mystical, non-literal image, it would produce meaning for audiences in unpredictable and uneven ways. Barthes distinguished the third mode from the second by the way it seemingly lacks a distinct code. If the second order of signification is cultural and literal, the third level is perceptual and symbolic. The perceptual message acts as a support for the other, more dependable modes of signification that cultural knowledge enables.

Barthes uses the word 'polysemy' to describe the interplay between the three orders of signification. The word suggests that the 'semiotic' powers of the image – its mechanical abilities to produce meanings for the spectator – are multiple, complex, and often difficult to disentangle. This semiotic trouble ensures that images are magical, extreme, or otherwise dysfunctional, especially when compared with the more straightforward fashion in which written words might disclose their meanings. In its complexity, the visual image is particularly prone to surprises of meaning, including the painful effect Barthes calls the 'punctum', in a later book on photography, *Camera Lucida* (1980). In images, a sign can strike the viewer where it hurts, causing a disturbing, unexpected experience that cannot easily be defined in intellectual terms. This is the punctum of the image. By refusing the 'studium' – the neutral content of an image that is seemingly available to all readers – the punctum bursts through the analytic screen of the image (p. 27). The punctum points to the seemingly magical relation between an image and what it does to sympathetic viewers. All images – performed or otherwise – possess a studium, but they may not inflict a punctum.

It is at the level of the punctum that Barthes' three orders of meaning are thrown into a crisis of signification, with 'magical' effects. In *The Scandal of Images* (2005), Marguerite Tassi explains that anxieties about vision in the early modern period were caused by a theory called 'intromission', which held that evil entered the soul through the body's apertures. Tassi cites Anthony Munday, who wrote in 1580, 'There cometh much evil in at the eares, but more at the eies [...] Nothing entereth more effectualie than that which cometh by seeing' (p. 18). This reading might strike the modern reader as quaint, but critics who rail against the corrupting potential of images stage similar anxieties to that voiced by Tassi's late-sixteenth-century fantasist. We can see a similar sensibility in more recent 'iconoclastic' responses to theatre, when moral crusaders like Mary Whitehouse or Senator Jesse Helms have attempted to limit the imagined threats posed by the punctum of a performed image.

Visual trouble

The trouble that performed images can cause is crucially dependent on the traditional assumptions of the historical moment in which one looks. In *Visuality in the Theatre* (2008), Maaike Bleeker argues that theatrical looking depends upon 'focalization' (p. 33), the physical positioning of one's body in relation to the thing seen. Other contingencies, such as race, class, sexuality, and gender, also condition the ways we orient ourselves towards an image. The particularities of vision are therefore complex: not only dependent on our 'subject position', but also historically and culturally specific. The effects of an image or other text can never be fixed objectively without disarming or obscuring its intrinsic status as a volatile and unstable phenomenon.

What does the way we view images tell us about the historical situations from which we look? How have new techniques of viewing, reading, and deciphering images affected the ways we understand ourselves as social, cultural, and political subjects? Visual studies scholars have frequently asked similar questions, but their inquiries have been directed more often towards art objects than towards theatre events. Theatrical images are implicated within the same conditions of meaning production as other technologies of visual representation, such as advertising, but also visual art, photography, dreaming, and other less obvious situations in which people produce and consume images. For the study of theatrical images, then, part of the 'problem' of the visual is that it seems to belong to other disciplines, including art history, visual studies, or the philosophical sub-discipline of aesthetics. If visual studies has often trained its gaze on works of art, its conclusions have had profound implications for other acts of seeing and being seen, from daily experience to the more culturally and socially specific exchanges of theatrical representation. The act of looking at art complements and extends the vernacular (or everyday) practices of looking at bodies, objects, and technological media, and being looked at by others, within what W. J. T. Mitchell calls the 'social field' of the visual (*What Do Pictures Want?* 2005, p. 365). Visual experience and social participation are deeply intertwined in his account, to the extent that the social construction of vision is inseparable from the visual construction of the social.

By highlighting the social construction of looking – the contingency of our ways of viewing the world – visual culture asks us to examine 'the strange things we do while looking, gazing, showing and showing off – or while hiding, dissembling, and refusing to look', as Mitchell writes (p. 356). Such activities certainly remind us of the peculiar acts of looking demanded in theatres. In theatre studies, the concept of 'theatricality' emphasises the fact that individual audience members bring a host of prejudices (against fakery or frivolity, for example), cultural assumptions and aspirations, identifications, and desires to the theatrical encounter. These particularities inevitably condition the way a work might produce meaning. Though this book is titled *Theatre & the Visual*, its two key themes must be considered in terms of theatricality and visuality, foregrounding the theatre and the visual as thoroughly contingent, historical phenomena.

Part One

histories of looking

A closer look at historical relations between theatre and the visual – or between theatricality and visuality – enables a counterintuitive account of theatrical experimentation and spectatorship. As vision is never simply a politically neutral act of looking at something 'given to be seen', we need to consider how historical developments have intruded upon visual experience in the theatre. I examine two revolutionary moments that reinvented Western scopic regimes in the fifteenth and nineteenth centuries. The invention of artificial perspective during the Italian Renaissance was the most ambitious and far-reaching event for the constitution of modern theories of vision. How did it affect the design of theatre spaces, and, by extension, the politics of theatrical representation? Four centuries later, how did the industrial provision of gas and electricity allow the development of modern technologies for lighting and looking in the theatre?

There are many other events that could be privileged in a fuller historical overview of the ways new technologies of vision have affected the scopic regimes of theatrical modernity. A different approach might have focused on the development of spectacle in historical theatres: baroque performance at Louis XIV's Versailles; festival spectacles at the Medici court; the Jacobean masques of Ben Jonson and Inigo Jones; or nineteenth-century sensation melodrama. In the nineteenth and twentieth centuries, technological innovation and 'new media' increasingly shifted general experiences of the visual in the theatre. For example, as the feminist film historian Linda Williams shows in *Hard Core: Power, Pleasure, and the 'Frenzy of the Visible'* (1999), the invention of cinema, as a new technology of vision, enabled new understandings of movement through slow-motion representation, and this affected understandings of gesture, as well as of the ways bodies were read by spectators in the late nineteenth century. A historicist approach shows that early cinema 'would produce a new kind of body, which viewers experience through this optical machine' (p. 45). Williams also shows that during the twentieth century, the forging of a relation between pornography and consumer capitalism brought further changes, including a general recognition of the centrality of sexist, racist, and homophobic gazes as organising principles within canonical visual representation. A different approach might investigate the development of digital media in the twentieth century, and their effects upon how we process visual material in the theatre (for a comprehensive analysis, see Bleeker's *Visuality in the Theatre*, pp. 146–59).

The invention of perspective

By disguising the social fact of visuality, scopic regimes naturalise the fiction of politically neutral vision, ordering contingent ways of seeing in an artificial hierarchy of visual styles. The central example of this situation – in which a means of looking is constructed and in turn naturalised – is the invention of artificial perspective in the fifteenth century. It constituted one of the key scopic revolutions, and paved the way for the visual techniques of modernity. The Italian Renaissance architect Filippo Brunelleschi invented artificial, or linear, perspective in a series of drawings around 1425. Perspective was a novel way of representing architectural and other objects, through a compositional system that imposed vanishing points and straight lines as rules for translating three-dimensional shapes into legible two-dimensional images.

Soon after Brunelleschi's exploratory drawings, perspective was theorised in a treatise called *On Painting* (1435), by the polymath Leon Battista Alberti. Alberti's model translates a visual field into uniform, symmetrical visual pyramids, whose tips point to and mirror the eye of the beholder. While perspective aspires to the status of an optically self-evident model of vision, it forces the arbitrary equivalence between a biological experience of sight (the way that the brain muddles divergent, partial sets of information provided by the eyes into a coherent image) and painting or drawing as conventional symbolic forms. In their realist modes, the latter constructs are assumed to be natural equivalents of less mediated, more direct visual experiences of the world.

Despite its appearance as a natural order of visual representation, artificial perspective is far from politically neutral. As Martin Jay notes in his 1988 essay 'Scopic Regimes of Modernity', Alberti's theory relies on the medieval conception of vision as an effect of divine illumination. By drawing lines between objects and the eye of the spectator, perspective suggested a harmonious relation between mathematical optics and visual representation as a manifestation of God's will.

After Alberti, vision was reconceptualised as a singular event, even though human vision is generally binocular. With the invention of perspective, Jay writes, the eye is 'understood to be static, unblinking, and fixated, rather than dynamic' (p. 7). This model of vision refuses mobility and duration, and imagines the act of looking as a type of epiphany – a singular manifestation of an eternal, immobile present, which can be reflected in symbolic forms such as painting and sculpture. As the religious overtones of 'epiphanic' vision subsided, the objective status of perspective as a scopic regime nevertheless remained in place. Perspective was an invention that quickly become hegemonic, which is to say that despite being devised as a new schema for architectural drawing and painting, it quickly acquired the status of an objective, natural logic of representation. For Jay, its implications were displaced from religious representations to the spatial relations that painters and draughtsmen used to depict all manners of visual effects. After the invention and naturalisation of artificial perspective, forms that are geometric, rectilinear, and uniformly constructed take on a kind of metaphysical (though secular) objectivity (pp. 5–7).

Artificial perspective re-imagined the painter's canvas as a transparent window onto the world. In the theatre, perspective hides its own artificiality by removing the screen that intervenes between the beholder and the image. However, the ways we process and understand what we see on the stage are deeply affected by the ascension of artificial perspective to the status of a natural or hegemonic order of vision. Literal adaptations or translations between works in different media – for example, paintings and theatrical representations – are described using the technical term *ekphrasis*. We can, however, see some less straightforward similarities between painting and theatre. Traditionally, the theatre reproduces the highly artificial position of the fixed viewer, defying the mobility of human vision by rooting each audience member in a static viewing position. Theatre auditoria were designed to privilege the perspective of the king, as an earthly representative of God's all-seeing eye.

Traditional set painting began to reproduce the perspectival illusionism of Renaissance painting – with painted flats, for example – often compounding this artificiality with theatrical illusionism. Character, narrative, and other dramatic constructs force similarities between what we see on the stage and how we exist in the world outside the theatre. Both models of illusionism produce and naturalise a conviction that the way we experience the world is rational, transparent, and orderly. Dramatic narrative often tends towards a linguistic approximation of the 'epiphanic' model of perspectival vision. Conflict is set up, developed, and resolved, through the agency of an author who traditionally sits outside of the work. The spectator models her or his reading by attempting to second-guess the supposedly singular, orthodox vision of the dramatist.

However, if artificial perspective formalised new understandings of vision, and suggested a transcendental, monocular subject position, innovators in the visual and dramatic arts were hardly bound to this model. Hans Holbein the Younger's *The Ambassadors* (1533) is the classic example of a painting that demonstrates the artificiality of perspectival vision, and the cohabitation of more than one style of looking in a single historical space (see figure 1). *The Ambassadors* requires the spectator to move below and to the left of the painting. When we look across the picture plane from this position, the anamorphic blur of grey, ochre, and black at the bottom of the painting coheres into a recognisable image of a human skull, as a *memento mori*, or reminder of mortality. Holbein's painting disturbs the singularity of vision that the rest of the composition seems to naturalise: the frontal representation of two men in ceremonial garb flanking an allegorical display of objects, including scientific instruments, a globe, and a lute. *The Ambassadors* stages an irreconcilable competition between divergent ways of seeing, as the spectator must shuttle – physically and conceptually – between divergent subject positions. In its use of anamorphosis, the painting suggests that in the place from which one looks, divergent practices of looking can be reconciled *theatrically* into a harmonious project. In this way, the painting

Figure 1   Hans Holbein the Younger, *The Ambassadors* (1533)
© The National Gallery, London. Used with permission.

gestures to a progressive, 'theatrical' model of vision, where an event is seen simultaneously from several perspectives.

'Perspective', here, refers to both the conceptual and physical positions from which a subject looks. As such, Holbein's *The Ambassadors* also suggests the corporeality of performance in both senses of perspective. By privileging the live body of the spectator over the static bodies represented in the painting, Holbein reminds us that the flesh is ennobling. The immobile bodies of the men of learning (represented in the painting) are caught in a missed encounter with the anamorphic skull in front of them. While painted bodies can never see, Holbein's ambassadors are doubly hindered, as the skull sits in a space that is profoundly disconnected from the picture plane in which they stand depicted. The painting suggests that mobility and physicality are important, human privileges: manifest, rather than represented. The ability to hold two contesting perspectives in tension is available only to the living bodies that behold the painting, in our partial, disorderly, yet thoroughly active attempts at exploration, cognition, and vision. This reminds us of the argument that the theatre produces and privileges active spectators, who must follow the movements of bodies, and other temporal elements of a stage production, and produce meaning from visual and other experiences. Much has been made of this active quality of theatrical vision, often in comparison to the relatively passive mode of vision that the other arts produce.

In his refusal of the stable, monocular subject position of artificial perspective, Holbein anticipates challenges to perspectivalism associated with painting in the late nineteenth and early twentieth centuries. These avant-garde innovations include the skewing and exaggeration of shapes and tones in expressionism, the overlapping and mobility of forms in cubism, and the breaking up of visual fields in impressionism. Holbein is a useful reminder that artists use experimental forms of visual representation (in his case, anamorphosis) to attack traditions in the heyday of their dominance. If vision itself has a history, it consists of the dominant models that have been devised and naturalised, and the subcultural, socially resistant challenges that artists have posed by experimenting with visual representation. By developing visual subcultures, artists remind the viewer that looking is always a historical, political act.

Moreover, the ways we are instructed to look are tied to possibilities that become available for politically active engagement. If the theatre has often fixed the viewer in the physical location from which she sees, it also necessitates a mode of viewing that relies upon a *mutual* situation of mobility: we look at a body that moves, and we identify with that capacity for movement. Holbein's painting cannot produce this event of reciprocal vision between two or more living bodies. Theatre often involves the potential for reciprocal vision (even if traditional theatre rarely acknowledges or capitalises upon this possibility).

Lighting and illusion

Visual culture suggests that a change in the way art is produced, understood, and valued can positively influence the social reality of the viewer's experience. The theatre is subject to a series of formative changes. What it means to be an audience is different from one historical moment to another. Due to the different social and technological conditions of theatrical production, the experience of 'looking' at the stage is shown to be radically contingent. Linking both of these changes, subsequent historical moments produce variations in the self-identity of audiences, who are invited to be 'transported' through involvement with a visual image.

Each new model of vision also coincides with – and is informed by – cultural, social, and other revolutions. Between the first theorisation of theatre lighting in the fifteenth century and the provision of gaslight in the 1820s and 1830s, artificial light was transformed from a technology that simply permits spectators to see into a sophisticated set of techniques for aiding the production of meaning in the theatre. In 1822, the technologically advanced illumination of the actor Edmund Kean prompted Samuel Taylor Coleridge to comment: 'To see him act is like reading Shakespeare by flashes of lightning' (cited in George Rowell's 1978 history of *The Victorian Theatre 1792–1914*, p. 24). Coleridge's poetic description of Kean's excesses is useful for the purposes of this discussion, as it compromises the status of a text by giving precedence to the experience of seeing a body on stage. In Coleridge's famous statement, the act of attending the theatre in the age of industrial lighting is rethought as a highly corporeal experience in which a spectator may struggle to decide whether looking or reading should take precedence. For Coleridge, the assumed purity of writing and reading is compromised by the new technologies that make the body and its gestures more readily available to vision.

The technological developments in lighting might suggest that theatrical vision underwent a historical development from its 'primitive' moment to a more advanced or civilised mode of visual experience. However, history can be shown to develop in surprising, non-linear, non-progressive ways, and the historical development of lighting can be seen as quite deeply troubled by the introduction of new technologies. Not simply a maturation of 'prehistoric' techniques, the new technologies were perceived variously as a hindrance, a nuisance, and an outright danger to the conventions of looking that the theatre depended upon.

Theatre lighting before the nineteenth century wasn't simply a primitive tool for seeing actors in darkened spaces. Theatre historian Tracy C. Davis observes continuities in the techniques used before and after the availability of gas and electricity. Davis notes the changes enabled by technological advances after the granting of a government charter for gaslight provision in 1812, writing that 'gaslight did not change the direction of light but greatly enhanced its intensity, with strong overhead and side lighting particularly instrumental in rounding out the figure of the actor in space' ('Reading Shakespeare by Flashes of Lightning', 1995, p. 934). Moreover, in *Theatre Lighting Before Electricity* (1978), Frederick Penzel shows that lighting had been used for complex aesthetic purposes (and not as merely a functional instrument) since the sixteenth century, when architects and artists of the Italian Renaissance, including Sebastiano Serlio and Nicola Sabbatini, invented new lighting techniques. Placing highly polished basins behind torches focused the glare into mobile spotlights. Passing light through *bozze* (glass containers filled with coloured liquids) produced coloured washes and spots. Footlights could be dimmed by lowering a row of cylinders over oil lamps using a pulley system (pp. 9–10). In England, pioneers appropriated the new methods after the restoration of the English monarchy in 1660, when King Charles II and his court returned from exile in France, bringing news of aesthetic achievements from continental Europe. Moreover, in the context of the English Restoration, when perspective scenery was introduced into public theatre, the question of an audience looking at the actor, and the latter looking back at the audience, became directly relevant.

Flammable gases were first collected for industrial purposes in the 1730s, but it was not until the turn of the following century that theatres cottoned onto the possibilities this innovation could offer as a technique for lighting productions. In 1804, the Lyceum Theatre in London was the first venue to demonstrate gas-powered lighting. In 1807, the National Light and Heat Company laid its first mains, and a royal charter in 1812 brought gas to the rest of London. This brought new possibilities for theatre lighting, for example the use of limelight (or calcium light) to illuminate an actor's body without brightening the surrounding space, leading to the development of the modern followspot. In the 1870s, when working as a lighting designer for the Lyceum Theatre, Bram Stoker (author of *Dracula*) noted that 'it became an easy matter to throw any special part of the stage into greater prominence' (cited in Penzel, *Theatre Lighting Before Electricity*, p. 61). New designs for lighting also meant that theatre artists could manipulate the mobility of spectators' visual experience. If in the eighteenth century the theatre became associated with the possibility of democratic politics, the newly theorised agency of the spectator was complemented in the following century by technological innovations.

Gas put new aesthetic conventions into play. With a *jeu d'orgue*, or gas table, the lights could be brought up easily on stage as the action commenced, and manipulated to create a broadened range of effects throughout the production. Audiences learnt to read these visual signs, imbuing dark and light in the theatre with new meaning. With increased brilliance and directionality, lights showed more of an actor's gestures and expressions, such that acting styles, oration, and make-up were eventually subdued to compensate for the advantages of greater visibility. Some visual distractions, including the candlesnuffer roaming the stage, and physical dangers, such as the hot wax that dripped from chandeliers onto audience members, were consigned to the dustbin of history.

However, if pre-industrial techniques had their problems, including difficulties in manipulating the intensity and direction of lighting, the introduction of gas intensified the hazards associated with theatre. Lighting a jet of gas produced from a coal-burning retort gave a brilliant light, but it also produced a noxious smell in the auditorium. This problem was compounded by other worrisome effects. As Penzel notes, audiences experienced 'a burning and prickling sensation in their eyes, a soreness in the throat, and a headache which lasted for several days' after each performance, as a result of oxygen depletion and the inhalation of toxic fumes such as carbonic acid (p. 42). Moreover, the temperature in the theatre would easily rise to 90°F (30°C). Health and safety anxieties led major venues such as London's Royal Coburg Theatre (now the Old Vic) to keep oil lamps until the late 1830s, when increased ventilation was shown to overcome the undesirable consequences of new techniques for theatre lighting.

In *The Archaeology of Knowledge* (1969), the French philosopher Michel Foucault writes, 'the history of a concept is not wholly and entirely that of its progressive refinement, its continually increasing rationality' (p. 4). Foucault encouraged new historicist approaches by disrupting the common-sense understandings of theoretical, industrial, and other types of evolution, as 'bold strokes [over] lines that have already been sketched'; in their place, he privileged the counterintuitive breaks that emerge when 'one is forced to advance beyond familiar territories, far from the certainties to which one is accustomed, towards an as yet uncharted land and unforeseeable conclusions' (p. 42). In terms of the advances brought by technological innovation in theatre lighting, an 'unforeseeable conclusion' is the peculiar way gas and electricity confirmed theatre's alignment with risk, danger, shock, and disaster.

Similarly, the commercial introduction of electric power in England in 1887 led to new transformations, as gaslight was phased out in favour of electricity. The visual possibilities of seeing improved, leading to what Jonathan Crary calls, in *Techniques of the Observer* (1990), 'a freeing up of vision' in the nineteenth century (p. 24). I argue that this produced amplified affective responses in audiences, such as laughter, discomfort, and fear. Joanna Bourke has even suggested a curious partnership between advances in electrical theatrical lighting and the cultural history of modern fear, after the colossal fires that killed hundreds in theatres in the early 1900s. The greatest theatre fire took place at the Iroquois Theatre in Chicago in 1903, when an electric floodlight ignited drapery and 600 people were killed (*Fear: A Cultural History*, 2005, pp. 51–52).

Electricity also enabled a series of shifts in the use and effects of theatrical illusion. In the seventeenth and eighteenth centuries, theatre vied with 'peculiar' or 'extraordinary entertainments' – popular performances by travelling show-persons, who presented tricks, illusions, sleights of hand, and other novelties to audiences. Harnessing the intrigue and fear inspired by emergent technologies in the years after Michael Faraday's touring exhibitions of the 1830s (in which the possibilities of electricity were brought to new audiences), entertainers such as Walford Bodie used electricity and its derivatives to modernise the longer-serving techniques of stage magic and illusion.

In eighteenth- and nineteenth-century England, audiences could witness acts of theatrical magic, including ventriloquism, contortion, prestidigitation (sleight of hand), escapology, and performances by 'learned' animals. The invention of electrical apparatus for the theatre offered new potentials for illusion. Billing himself as 'The Electric Wizard' or 'The British Edison' in the 1890s, Bodie would electrocute himself and volunteers on stage, and audiences would gasp and stare at the spectacle of bodies contorted by (electrostatic) currents. A contemporary critic noted, 'As the current increases, each person will be more or less grotesque, and most laughable to behold' (cited in Jay, 1986, p. 128). In *Learned Pigs and Fireproof Women* (1986), a history of stage illusion, Ricky Jay describes other tricks. Bodie would invite a pair of lovers to each hold a wire handle connected to a large electromagnetic coil; as the lovers moved their faces together to kiss, a shock of bright electric current would pass through the air between their puckered lips. Other volunteers would attempt to retrieve a coin from an electrified bucket of water, or be shocked in mock electric chairs, with amusing results (pp. 127–29).

As Bodie's 'low' theatre showed, the introduction of new technologies had far-reaching influences on theatrical representation in the nineteenth century, not simply for new formal and aesthetic lighting techniques, but also for the production of illusion on stage. In conflict with the familiar assumption that new lighting techniques simply brought actors and their actions into plainer view, technological innovations in fact produced a broader set of cultural shifts. These included the alignment between visual experience in the theatre and a host of potent effects – and affects – including risk, disaster, laughter, and fear.

In summary, technological advances were not simply incidental to the theatre, but enabled new trends and conventions, in the institutional spaces of theatrical representation, and at its subcultural margins. The improvements and appropriations furnished by artificial perspective and new sources of power such as gas and electricity had far-reaching effects on the development of the performed image, producing political agency in audiences, and inciting new affective investments in theatrical spectatorship. These and other elements would be confirmed as key aspects of theatre in the twentieth century, as the primacy of the word was challenged by new ways of emphasising the cultural effects of visuality.

Part Two

wordless spectacle

I n the last one hundred years, theatre has involved a series of challenges to the supposed primacy of textual production over other forms of representation. Since the early twentieth century, some theatre artists have refused the spoken word in performance to decentre the idea of theatre as a literary form. These efforts have troubled the authority of the text, and celebrated the effects of process, contingency, failure, and participation. How do these shifts relate to and condition visual experience in performance? How do words – those of audiences, critics, or historians – enter to fill the gap created by the displacement of the text by visual phenomena? How do we read theatrical works that consist solely of images, or that interrupt the narrative play of texts with striking visual interludes? By asking these and other questions, I take a closer look at intersections between theatre and visual culture. I argue that as contemporary theatre moves away from the primacy of the play text, and towards the orchestration of performed images, it stages and exceeds the pioneering visual developments of theatrical modernism.

Unmooring the theatrical event from its dependency on the dramatic text gives rise to new strategies for the production of meaning in performance. Specifically, I argue that when theatre artists abandon the spoken word in performance, audiences are encouraged to invent new ways of producing meaning in our encounters with the challenges posed by wordless spectacle. In terms of this strategy, the work of the British-based performance artist Franko B is exemplary. His most celebrated works have employed bloodletting in visually compelling settings. In his visceral performances, the audience is encouraged to read the body and its biological processes as something other than straightforward symbols or metonyms. Moreover, his work asks each audience member to privilege her or his affective relationship with the artist's body, and to reassess assumptions about consent, vulnerability, dignity, and political agency.

By highlighting the fact of its own mediated condition, performance art invites us to reflect upon the experience of being the subject of vision, in art and everyday life. The particularities of the spectator's identity affect how it feels to be the subject of reciprocal vision, in performance, but also in other social situations. The challenges involved in staging wordless spectacle have been a crucial aspect of the encounter with performance art, at least since the 1960s, yet have also troubled the encounter with dramatic arts since much earlier in the twentieth century. For example, the modernist innovations of Antonin Artaud in the 1930s, and the plays of Jean Genet, Eugene Ionesco, and Samuel Beckett in the 1940s and 1950s, include highly visual elements, often alongside challenging texts. Beckett's *Breath* (Eden Theater, New York, 1969) condensed this history into a short, sharp play without words. It consists of a sequence of images and sounds, but the latter do not approach the linguistic directness of the spoken word. The play begins with a faint light rising on the stage to reveal a scatter of domestic rubbish. After five seconds, a brief recording of a faint cry is heard. A long recorded intake of breath rises in volume in tandem with a slow blaze of light. The sound and light reach a maximum, followed by a short burst of silence. The auditorium fills with the sound of an expulsion of breath, which decreases to silence with the synchronised lowering of the light. A further cry is heard in the dark, followed by silence. The performance lasts around 40 seconds.

Beckett's work is highly relevant to a discussion of the relation between theatre and the visual, as he integrates scenography – the visual elements of the theatre from the static and pictorial design of a production to more complicated lures to the spectator's activity of looking – into his play texts. In *The Cambridge Introduction to Scenography* (2009), Joslin McKinney and Philip Butterworth note that other playwrights, including Arthur Miller and Tennessee Williams, also collaborated with scenographers during the direction and production of their plays; however, they add, Beckett anticipated the visual scenarios of his theatre, opposing the tendency for traditional dramatic arts to 'typically separate the work of the playwright from the actual production of the play text' (p. 83). Beckett's plays fix the visual aspects of his theatre, and since his death in 1989 his estate has rigorously enforced the visual constraints he wrote into his plays.

Moreover, *Breath* is a remarkable distillation of theatre into the image. It was a progressive challenge to the dominance of the word, and opposed the authority of sense and rationality in dramatic literature and the performing arts. Although *Breath* excludes the image of the performing body, the event still provides plenty of opportunities for creative reflection upon the terms and conditions of bodily interaction. While the emphasis on breath seems to suggest the processes of life, the absenting of bodies from the boisterous blankness of the stage suggests the impossibility of survival. The visual world of Beckett's *Breath* seems to imagine a subtle death. If it augurs an apocalyptic future, this is relieved by laughter because the work itself barely achieves the status of theatrical representation.

The loss of speech to vision

What is at stake in the loss of speech to vision? I suggest a series of relationships between looking, speaking, and thinking, and argue that experimental performance can be explored to shed some light upon the role of each. In March 2003, Franko B presented his iconic performance *I Miss You* in the Turbine Hall, a cavernous space in the Tate Modern, London. As Franko B walks up and down a canvas catwalk, blood seeps from hypodermic sleeves inserted into veins in the crooks of his elbows. As he marches gently past the hushed audience members, blood drips down his arms, pools in and around his fingers, and splashes down his legs to the canvas beneath his feet. As our gazes shift between his eyes and his open wounds, he holds us in tense reciprocal stares.

In *I Miss You*, Franko B challenges the tradition of the performer who is rarely, in practice, asked to look back at the audience. Indeed, actors are seldom able to, as conventional stage lighting blinds them from seeing the auditorium. In traditional theatre, the performer is therefore a peculiarly antisocial figure: the situations in which actors perform approximate reciprocal relations, yet they usually feign participation in a social contract; situations rarely arise in which a visual exchange can be achieved as a properly relational encounter. As Rebecca Schneider writes in her essay 'On Taking the Blind in Hand', an actor's refusal extends to the metaphorical 'blindness' of characters:

> [T]he actor does not see – he, often together with his character, does not see his future, though it is the very scripted future the audience has come to watch played out. At least the actor pretends not to see. He agrees to be blinded, just as the audience agrees not to act. (pp. 26–27)

Schneider suggests that the 'blindness' of actors mirrors the customary refusal of spectators to intervene physically in the situations they witness. Both customs produce oddly depoliticised variations on social realities outside the theatre.

In performance art, however, the artist often returns the spectator's look with conviction; the spectator is often called upon to act on her or his political or ethical convictions. Each *potentially* responds as a subject of free will. In such cases, the scene of looking opens onto political possibilities that may not be available in the traditionally more tightly constrained theatrical setup.

In some performances, spectators act upon their desires in profoundly active ways. In Franko B's works, our situation of looking is subtler, partly because his destitution frequently strips us of our ability to conceptualise his image in convivial terms. In Jennifer Doyle's emotive response to *I Miss You*, the emotional weight of reciprocal vision gives rise to a feminist reappraisal of the politics of performance. She describes the 'critical tears' she wept while watching, and suggests that when audiences write about his works, 'we stumble over our own feelings – and over the discomfort they pose, especially for the critic' ('Critical Tears', 2006, p. 43). The artist remains silent, and looking on we may find ourselves at a temporary loss for words. Words, it seems, fail to fill the space left by the absenting of performed speech. For Doyle, part of the challenge of visually powerful performances is the way they inaugurate an emotional loss of words in audiences.

Part of this devastation emerges from the uniqueness of the social relation that such performances produce. Although the spectacle on stage might seem 'unmediated', or might remind us of interpersonal relations outside the theatre, performance is always of a different order to actual interactions on the world stage. Franko B belongs to a long history of artists who have used the body in carefully staged ('mediated') events while departing from the traditional legacies of theatrical performance. In abandoning the fakery associated with acting, Franko B nevertheless plays on the familiar disasters feigned in tragic drama: the wounds that characters endure for their failings, and that signify vulnerability or doomed futures. Even when a performance artist abandons the spoken word – upon which much of the theatrical production of meaning has been assumed to rest – the trappings of the theatre can be seen to survive in the performed image. Theatre enacts a visual return, precisely in the spaces from which it has been strategically displaced.

Wordless interruptions

The elevation of the visual aspects of theatre to new heights is a strategy that owes much of its charge to the theorisations of the theatrical avant-garde, and especially to the writings of Antonin Artaud. In his celebrated text 'Theatre and the Plague' (1938), Artaud writes:

> The plague takes dormant images, latent disorder and suddenly carries them to the point of the most extreme gestures. Theatre also takes gestures and develops them to the limit [...]. For theatre can only happen the moment the inconceivable really begins, where poetry taking place on stage, nourishes and superheats created symbols. (p. 18)

While such assaults are readily associated with recent performance art, the return to Artaud's theories assimilates the assault on vision to more traditional histories of theatrical performance. David Bradby and Annie Sparks write that the distillation of the visual potential of theatre was a strategic starting point for practitioners in France in the mid-twentieth century. Playwrights such as Beckett, Genet, and Ionesco, and companies such as Théâtre du Soleil, 'rejected the familiar drama of rational debate or conversation in favour of raw images making a direct assault on the sensibilities of their *spectateurs*' (*Mise en Scène*, 1997, p. xxiii). By using the French word for audience, Bradby and Sparks imply that different cultures variously emphasise the visual or auditory experiences of performance.

Engineering an assault upon the senses was a central project for the historical avant-garde, and has been continued by practitioners of experimental theatre, live art, and performance art. As a form that explores the cultural work performed by visual representation, theatre arts are not simply means of bringing texts to life. Instead, the theatre becomes a medium – or a set of related media – typified by the production of live images, often alongside other effects such as communal, social, or reciprocal experience, choreographed movement, technological mediation, and the delivery of texts, music, and other sound scores.

Since the twentieth century, playwrights and theatre artists have also emphasised the power of the performed image to provoke audiences in plays consisting mostly of recited speech. After the abolition of censorship in the theatre, with the passing of the Theatres Act 1968, British theatre cleaved to situations where visual experimentation might provoke audiences, but frequently relieved of the age-old threat of legal prosecution. As suggested in my intro-duction, In-Yer-Face Theatre plays such as Sarah Kane's *Blasted*, Anthony Neilson's *Penetrator*, and Mark Ravenhill's *Shopping and Fucking* made much of the power of the visual to unsettle theatrical audiences. Often the conventions of theatrical representation were distilled in these plays into thickly constructed visual images.

In *Penetrator*, for example, Neilson's short scenes of violence-addled interactions follow a troublingly stark pro-logue in which a man stands with his thumb out, engulfed by the sounds of rain and the occasional passing car. Sets of headlights illuminate his hopeless wait by the drama-tised roadside. An inhuman, rumbling voice-over narrates a long, crude pornographic fantasy: 'She hitched up her tiny skirt to reveal her gash, spreading the lips of her fuck-hole like some filthy tart, a flood of thick cunt juice cascading down her long legs. She sobbed with pleasure,' the narra-tor adds bathetically (p. 61). Neilson and his contemporaries dramatised – or rather, visualised – the nation as a grim accumulation of failed subjects in a landscape of human degradation. In such instances, the physiological situation of feeling at a loss opens audiences up to a range of compensa-tory responses, including indignation, fear, threat, disgust, or embarrassment, as variations on the climactic indignity of looking at the unfamiliar. The bleak visual effect references the condensation of event and action in Beckett's *Breath*,

and Artaud's call to reinvent the theatre as 'the exterior-
isation of a latent undercurrent of cruelty' ('Theatre and
the Plague', p. 21). By questioning the primacy of the text,
in wordless, visual interruptions, the theatre draws on the
legacies of the avant-garde attack on the senses. By bridging
the visual and the textual in confrontational ways, theatre
perhaps appears more readily as a mode of production that
reflects the cultural, political, and intellectual preoccupa-
tions of the twenty-first century, even if the most challenging work seems to risk transforming the theatre into an
atrocity exhibition.

Part Three

the pleasures and pains of looking

'I'm a ward of the state of beauty,' writes the poet Eileen Myles. 'Even as it rots & corrupts [...] I still have to watch' (*Not Me*, 1991, p. 200). Similarly, a central characteristic of the works introduced in the previous sections is their need to push spectatorship to reassess the conventions of visual pleasure, and to consider the necessarily painful or disturbing experiences of looking at objects and bodies. I begin this section with an examination of the seemingly 'magical' effects that accompany visual pleasure in the theatre. When we look at the surfaces of things, including the bodies of performers, a number of pleasurable experiences seem to be implicated in spectatorship. However, with pleasure comes politics. I argue that the concept of fetishism is central to the production of meaning in the visual encounter, and I do so by explaining two theoretical accounts of this dynamic. I ask how relations of power might condition visual experience in the theatre, and how fetishism might also influence the pleasure of looking in surprising ways.

I draw on the theoretical achievements of psychoanalytic and Marxist analysis. Through discussions of the work of the theatre artist Neil Bartlett and the performance artist Annie Sprinkle, I ask how sexual minorities and women have used performance to expose, critique, and reorient the objectifying tendencies of vision in theatre and performance.

The magic of the image

Where there is pleasure in an image, there is magic: the flash of inspiration that accompanies or confuses a set of work processes. Moreover, where there is magic, there is fetishism. Fetishism was recognised as a crucial theoretical logic in the late nineteenth and early twentieth centuries, in two distinct (but similarly canonical) traditions of thought, Marxism and Freudian psychoanalysis. Its meanings are drawn from anthropological studies of the function of totems in non-Western cultures. In *Totemism and Exogamy* (1910), the social anthropologist James Frazer argued that the totemic structure was the basis for a bond much stronger than the bond of blood or family in the modern sense (p. 53). An object that stands as a point of reference for a society, the totem – often a guardian spirit, helper, or oracle, taking such forms as a totemic pole, crucifix, or other icon – is a magical emblem that conditions and also overrides the basic rituals of social participation. As an image that somehow forms the basis for – yet also exceeds – social relations, the fetish is of interest in the theatre, where highly coded social rituals are carried out to produce events that are consumed by groups of people. The pleasure these events produce is in some ways dependent on obscuring what Marxists call the material conditions of production: the relatively mundane situations, practices, and types of labour that a theatrical production relies on to come to fruition. When a theatrical image is understood as the effect of workaday processes – fundraising, rehearsal, blocking, directing, and so on – it loses some of the transcendent quality that is sometimes attached to art. The theatrical image becomes demystified, which troubles the smooth production of pleasure.

The legacies of fetishism are important because they allow us to rethink our exertions to make sense of inter-actions with visual culture. Performance and visual culture can train the eye, and revise the values we ordinarily ascribe to objects of vision. These acts of looking are necessarily difficult, even costly in a psychic sense, regardless of whether the effects they produce are pleasurable or painful. Demystification requires some level of complication of the ordinary processes of looking; it is less likely to arise when one engages in happy acts of looking. As the psychoanalytic theorist Jacqueline Rose argued in her seminal collection *Sexuality in the Field of Vision* (1986), highly charged acts of looking show that identification is paradoxical, because 'the subject finds or recognises itself through an image which simultaneously alienates it, and hence, potentially confronts it' (p. 174).

For Karl Marx, fetishism is an explicitly economic theory of objects and social relations. It refers to the alchemy of capitalism by which a common substance is transformed into a commodity. In Marx's celebrated essay 'The Fetishism of Commodities' (1867), capitalism forces a social relation between new forms of labour and the products of industry. The transformation is alchemical or 'mysterious', for Marx, because immaterial, social relations (making, selling, buying) take on objective status, in the form of a commodity that bears more power than the sum of its parts. In Marxist terminology, advanced capitalism complements the inherent 'use-value' or utility of an object with the attribution of 'exchange-value'. Commodities are not the natural placeholders for social relations, Marx writes in 'The Fetishism of Commodities', but are distinctly magical, because their values somehow exceed their physical properties and the material relations arising from them (p. 436). For example, a manufactured coat becomes more valuable as an object of exchange – a fetish – than simply the sum of its constituent parts of fabric, buttons, and threads. Branded goods acquire more value than unbranded goods – as if by magic. However, in this fetishistic or magical transformation, the labourer becomes devalued, or even dehumanised, by the processes of industrial (as opposed to 'organic') labour.

Similar to the language associated with the social power of the totem, the fetishism of commodities is 'superstitious' because it is an arbitrary and mysterious effect of industrial production. In other words, capitalism distorts a social convention – the way that man-made objects achieve an immaterial social character through exchange – by re-presenting value as a natural effect of objects. The ordinary objects of production are transformed into 'social hieroglyphics' which we then decipher or read as consumers, in ingenious attempts to 'get behind the secret' of capitalist consumption (p. 427). Art objects are powerful fetishes in the Marxist sense: a work that carries an aesthetic signature (a sort of brand or hieroglyph) is more expensive, and confers power upon its owner or the venue in which it is presented. Moreover, the importance of the art object – as a commodity *par excellence* – is calculated through secret, magical systems of valuation. As Wendy Steiner writes in *The Scandal of Pleasure* (1995), if we read the work of art through the prism of the fetish, 'we realize that the work takes on its special value because its audience treats it in a special manner – makes it into a fetish – and not because the work "contains" this value' (p. 81).

In visual art forms where objects are neither produced nor entered into circulation, as in most types of performance, the role of fetishism is even more pronounced. It is even clearer that 'superstitious' effects are at work, because a social relation between producer and consumer is being magically endowed with value. This process of valuation can be called 'cultural capital' – where attending a particular performance confers a sense of entitlement or achievement upon the consumer/spectator. In commercial theatre, the pleasure of visiting performances is sometimes confirmed or amplified by the purchase of a souvenir, such as a printed programme or other visual token of one's investment. Theatre and performance always put the logic of fetishism into play, because a value is appended to a system of relationships between individuals and actions.

Sigmund Freud's slightly later account of the power of fetishism is likewise a theory of objects and social relations. However, his 'magical' objects are stand-ins for profoundly erotic relations. Freud's account of fetishism is a psychoanalytic theory of vision, which accounts for the muddles that occur when we look from blighted positions and ascribe meaning and value where they scarcely seem to belong. Freudian fetishism is a troubled compensation for traumatic acts of looking. It is a mechanism of repression, specifically the variant Freud calls 'disavowal', which takes the silent form of the statement 'I know very well that something is the case, but I shall act otherwise'. Freud writes that fetishism emerges as a magical act of self-preservation in response to the male subject's overwhelming childhood trauma of realising that his mother lacks a penis. The mother's penis, Freud writes in 'Fetishism' (1927), 'should normally have been given up [to the castrating father], but the fetish is precisely designed to preserve it from extinction' (p. 352). Why not give it up? Castration anxiety (the founding Freudian myth) is the cause of the child's fetishistic horror, as the mother's lack is displaced onto a fear that the father will castrate the boy, and prevent him from attaining 'phallic' (full) subjectivity. 'In later life', Freud explains, 'a grown man may perhaps experience a similar panic when the cry goes up that Throne and Altar are in danger, and similar illogical consequences will ensue.'

The consequence for the fetishist is that he will transplant a powerful object in the place of the offending vagina, the apparent trace of the woman's castration. This fantasy

is a psychic compromise between a realisation ('I know ...')
and the counter-wish ('but ...'). Magical power (*cathexis*)
attaches itself to the substitute (the fetish), and its erotic
charge is ensured. In a superstitious process, 'the horror
of castration [sets] up a memorial to itself in the creation
of this substitute' – for example, a conventional object of
erotic investment such as women's underwear, high-heeled
shoes, or leather (p. 353). In *Hard Core*, Linda Williams
usefully summarises the fetishist's visual assertion. In the
(traumatic) grip of an erotic encounter, for example when
watching hardcore pornography, the fetishist invests in the
substitute, and makes the unconscious claim 'This [wom-
an's] body is not really so different from mine; it is not cas-
trated; here is the fetish that proves it' (p. 82).

Williams has explored extensively the problems Freud
poses for feminist analysis. A key limitation of Freud's
account is that his fetishists are necessarily male; however,
they are never homosexual. For Freud, male subjects choose
one of three possible solutions to the ubiquitous vaginal terror: they overcome it through 'normal' attempts at phallic
triumph and masculine exertion, or they settle for either of
two 'pathological' outcomes, namely fetishism (producing a
penis substitute) or homosexuality (valorising the penis and
ignoring the vagina altogether). The misogyny and homo-
phobia of Freud's account of women's bodies and of homosexuality are self-evident.

There are clear differences and similarities between the
Marxist and Freudian accounts of fetishism. Whereas Marx
gives an account of a universal process of mystification

under capitalism, Freud's fetishism is pathological, marginal, or subcultural. Nevertheless, both understand fetishism as an event of translation or misinterpretation — a wilful act of misreading that the subject undertakes to exploit the magical powers of objects. For Marx and Freud, the fetish is an object before which the supposed rationality of post-Enlightenment subjectivity comes unstuck. Both are theories of perception that account (in partial, conflicted ways) for the strategies we deploy to overcome the holes in our understandings of the roles we play in social relations.

Looking for the fetish

Freud's and Marx's theories are not interpretive tools: they neither reveal the 'truth' of theatre nor disclose a 'message' hidden away within the dark recesses of a performed image. Rather, they suggest how the fetish — as a theory of the magic of the image — conditions the way we look at objects and bodies in the theatre. Through two examples, I ask how performance practitioners have used the theatre to resist, exploit, or uncover the various logics of fetishism. Critical of the normative or conventional ways we look at bodies, some performance makers have produced pleasurable scenes of looking that require political transformations of vision. In the work of Neil Bartlett and Annie Sprinkle, new images broker pleasurable effects, by calling into question the paradoxical processes of identification, confrontation, and alienation that Jacqueline Rose observes. Marxist and Freudian analyses trouble the way in which these images

produce pleasure, encouraging complex attempts to demystify the power afforded to certain acts or images.

Neil Bartlett is a key figure in the development of queer
culture in Britain. Since the early 1980s, he has consistently moved between mainstream and marginal contexts
of artistic production. His works are preoccupied with
lost moments of lesbian and gay history, and often drama-
tise their powerful reanimation in the present. Bartlett is
an ideal case study for thinking about fetishism because
he consistently returns to the meaning that emerges from
situations of productive misreading, when two historical
situations are compared or richly conflated. *Or You Could
Kiss Me* was presented at the National Theatre in London in
November 2010, in collaboration with Handspring Puppet
Company. Bartlett's concern for the ways a history is cas-
ually lost, or deliberately scrubbed out, is dramatised in
the love story of two South African men as they prepare
for imminent death and remember events from the history
of their romance. Uncannily constructed puppets play the
lovers, and actors manipulate their wooden bodies through
the space of the theatre.

Puppetry is a popular form of visual theatre, which complements Bartlett's interest in tensions between high and
low theatrical cultures. Puppets are objects that undergo
magical or alchemical transformations in the space of performance. The puppet-bodies of the two protagonists are
relevant to a consideration of Marx's theory of the fetishism of commodities, as the puppet is very clearly an object
that stands in for a social relation. Whereas the commodity

is more commonly thought of in terms of economic transactions, the puppet-as-commodity in *Or You Could Kiss Me* produces an erotic transaction. Bartlett's play initiates an economy of desire in which audience members find themselves in the curious position of investing attention in the relationships between two objects of vision – inanimate objects that are seemingly in love. We watch the gentle rise and fall of the puppets' exhausted breath, the collapse of the puppets into bed, into a wheelchair, or into each other's arms. As a frail, elderly puppet looks through old photographs, his younger, athletic puppet-self bursts into the space, naked but for swimming trunks, and swims through the scene to emerge from water at the edge of an imaginary pool. The contrast is jarring, and the visual effect is disconcertingly erotic. The confusion is compounded by the fact that the puppet-handlers remain in plain sight, yet slip in and out of our cognition as we focus on the play.

The visual elements of Bartlett's theatre produce pleasurable inversions: the spectator's desires shuttle between a visual investment in objects (the puppets) and vicarious identifications with the difficult relations they represent (the lives of two gay men in apartheid-era South Africa). As fetish, the puppet both conceals and emphasises a social relation – 'a tenderness which was uncommon', in Tennessee Williams' evocative phrase – by pleasurably securing a place for a forgotten or marginal history within mainstream institutional culture. While under capitalism the fetishism of commodities is troubling – because it suppresses a social relation – in the theatre the 'superstitious' correspondence

between an object and its pleasurable effects can be politically enabling. Whereas a relationship is obscured in the
former, the theatre can allow for a social relation to be pas-
sionately articulated. This troubles the idea that analysis –
demystification – unsettles the production of pleasure. In
Bartlett's theatre, pleasure is amplified when we investigate
the techniques by which an effect is produced.

Like Bartlett's, Annie Sprinkle's performance work is
crucially important to the development of identity politics. Also like Bartlett, Sprinkle shuttles between marginal
and mainstream cultures with politically interesting effects.
Sprinkle is a former porn star and sex worker who turned
to performance art and sex education in the early 1980s.
Her best-known performance is *Annie Sprinkle, Post-Porn
Modernist* (The Kitchen, New York, 1989), which includes
an illustrated lecture on her porn career, audience participation, and vignettes such as 'A Public Cervix Announcement',
where audience members are invited to mount the stage to
look at her cervix, through a speculum inserted into her
vagina, lit by a handheld flashlight. Other similarly evocative
scenes include '100 Blow Jobs', in which she fellates a cache
of dildos mounted on a board, to the sound of abusive language uttered by former johns, and a 'sex magic' masturba-
tion ritual. In an interview with Andrea Juno, she describes
her work as a concerted effort to bring together sex, pleasure, and education in a performance context: 'There's so
much pain and suffering in the world that my purpose in life
is to have as much pleasure as possible – to be in perpetual
pursuit of pleasure' ('Annie Sprinkle', 1991, p. 28).

The Freudian account of fetishism is patently relevant to a consideration of Sprinkle's work, not least for her performance attire, which often includes a corset, uplift bra, stockings and garter belt, thigh-high boots with six-inch heels, and a welter of make-up on her smiling face. In a photographic work called *Anatomy of a Pinup* (1991), Sprinkle annotates the effects she employs to give her the perfect porn-star presentation, from her 'pucker [that] gives suggestion of a blow job' to the catalogue of implements that transform her body into that of a cartoon pinup. In Freud's anatomy of fetishism,

> the subject's interest comes to a halt half-way, as it were; it is as though the last impression before the uncanny and traumatic one is retained as a fetish. Thus [for example,] the foot or shoe owes its preference as a fetish – or part of it – to the circumstance that the inquisitive boy peered at the woman's genitals from below, from her legs up. (p. 354)

For Freud, the apparent horror of seeing a woman's genital 'lack' is substituted by the pleasure that preceded it, for the spectator, in a traumatic attempt at preventing the disastrous effects of his visual experience. The visual language of Freudian fetishism is played out in pornography, and in Sprinkle's performances. However, rather than merely illustrating the Freudian account and its shortcomings (for example, the assumption that women are not capable of sexual fetishism), Sprinkle's work raises interesting questions about the ways performance offers scenes in which the body can be reclaimed from oppressive visual logics. It gestures to the ways in which even a pleasurable visual experience might hide traumatic narratives, and suggests that the theatre is a supple mode of addressing the abuses of the past.

A straightforward response to 'A Public Cervix Announcement' might suggest that Sprinkle's work is complicit in misogynistic relations of power, where the woman's body is exploited as an object of vision – and, for Freud, as a *traumatic* one. However, Sprinkle effectively refuses the traditional assumption that a woman's body becomes 'objectified' – transformed into a controllable object – under the audience's gaze. By directing the view of the audience onto and into her body, Sprinkle reveals a part of her body (the cervix) that almost always escapes everyday, cinematic, or theatrical vision. By revealing a concealed image, Sprinkle appropriates and overturns a traumatic social relation, namely the dynamics of power that objectify and denigrate women. The object of vision, here, cannot simply function as a stand-in for oppressive relations of power (between men, over women). The visual element of Sprinkle's performance disrupts the Freudian myth of fetishism. She produces pleasurable refusals that short-circuit the traditional (pornographic) relationship between the viewer and the object of vision, because she cajoles viewers into modes of visual experience that demystify the hidden recesses of her body, while also being reciprocally pleasurable.

The theatre historian Rebecca Schneider has written of Sprinkle's work as a series of dialectical images: objects of vision that make the viewer look again to seek out the complexities in an image with two sides that cannot be easily reconciled. 'A Public Cervix Announcement' is a good example of a work that is 'at once exceedingly private, full of located and personal particulars of reading, and radically public', that is, 'socially inscribed' with conventional associations that inevitably permeate the act of looking. In *The Explicit Body in Performance* (1997), Schneider illustrates this dialectical model by reading Sprinkle's cervix as a 'theoretical third eye, like a gaze from the blind spot, meeting the spectator's – my – gaze' (pp. 53–55). As a 'counter-gaze', the 'look' returned by Sprinkle's body draws upon the scene of reciprocal vision that the theatre often thrives on.

Seeing in multiple and playful ways, Sprinkle is not blinded to the political complexities of her value as fetish, nor is she merely an unconflicted object of visual pleasure. Her body cannot be reduced to the objectifying, voyeuristic, exploitative social relation associated with mainstream pornography, even though her imagery is explicitly appropriated from the genre. Fetishism is marshalled into the theatrical situation of looking, but this 'magical' effect is troubled and exceeded by the image Sprinkle creates in performance. For Schneider, the image is 'dialectical' because it cannot be finally resolved. A certain tension resides in the scene in which one's look is directed by a smiling Sprinkle into the depths of her vagina. The result is a pleasurably 'fraught' scene of looking, which remains meaningfully

incomplete, politically ambiguous, and rich for interpret-
ation because of the untenable positions she seems to take
up in relation to the sexual politics of the theatre. The process returns us to the shortcomings of the Freudian account
of fetishism, and attempts to reclaim bodies from the history of violent transactions, where women have often been
the objects of oppressive acts of visual pleasure.

The scorched eye

Sprinkle's work is visually familiar, in terms of the imagery
she traffics into her performances. It is also visually alien,
because the bodies, objects, and histories she asks us to look
at are not self-determined when shown in theatrical venues. This central tension – between the everyday and the
exotic – derives from the political heart of avant-garde culture in the twentieth century. Avant-garde artists promoted
'defamiliarisation' – Bertolt Brecht's *Verfremdungseffekt* –
as a crucial strategy for shifting the political economy of
looking. A strategy of defamiliarisation surprises the viewer
out of socially conditioned ways of looking at art and, by
extension, at the world. Central to the history of the avant-
garde is the development of Dada and surrealist visual art
in France. For the proto-surrealist philosopher Georges
Bataille, writing in 1929, the eye is a 'cutting edge' between
the limits of seductiveness and 'the often inexplicable acuity
of horror' ('The Eye', p. 17). The eye is the human organ
that seemingly registers horror most viscerally and inescap-
ably; its representation as the object of pain or injury has a
peculiar capacity to invoke disgust or squeamishness. This

twin sensitivity to horror is convincingly demonstrated in a notorious scene from Salvador Dalí and Luis Buñuel's surrealist film *Un Chien Andalou* (1929), in which a cutthroat razor appears to slice across and into a woman's eyeball (actually a pig's eyeball, suggestively cut into a shot of a razor held against the face of actress Simone Mareuil).

Texts that demand careful political negotiations often draw the eye towards scenes that are difficult to apprehend. From canonical texts such as Sophocles' classical Greek play *Oedipus Rex* and Shakespeare's *King Lear* through to more recent 1990s plays such as Kane's *Blasted* or Neilson's *Penetrator*, the pain entailed in looking has been a persistent theme in the history of theatre. In these four dramatic fictions, for example, being 'a ward of the state of beauty' (in Eileen Myles' words) necessitates the surprising central event of gouged, injured, or obliterated eyes. The intensification of effects in the latter two works derives from the avant-garde project described above. Under the avant-garde influence, experimental theatre and performance art have upheld the project of defamiliarising how we look at objects and events, producing situations where looking becomes a painful action. Foremost among those who have achieved this cultural project of troubling the event of theatrical looking is the performance artist Ron Athey.

In performance, Athey stages painful actions that foreground the eye as a particularly vulnerable point of entry; he prioritises the physiologically challenging qualities of looking at a body in the grip of pain. In a *Guardian* article, journalist Lyn Gardner wrote of his recent 'savage, eye-scorching performance' *Self-Obliteration* (National Review of Live Art, Glasgow, 2010), 'For those of us who watch – or bear witness, as it so often feels in Athey's performances – it is as if he is trying to obliterate our vision of him' ('National Review of Live Art', 2010). Other reviewers similarly emphasised the intensity of vision when watching his performance. Also in the *Guardian*, the theatre director Tim Etchells suggested his difficulty in watching the same performance, and noted the untrustworthiness of vision and its subjugation to desire or anxiety in the theatre:

> Of the rumours [about Athey's piece] witnesses agree to disagree about pretty much everything: the quantities of blood spilled, whether it was deliberate or accidental, the number of punters who fainted, the exact range and trajectory of the crimson parabola that spurted from a wound in his scalp (or forehead or eyes). ('National Review of Live Art Meets a Bloody End')

In the performance at the National Review of Live Art, Glasgow, which I also attended, Athey is positioned on all fours on a high rostrum, naked except for a long golden wig that falls over his face and nearly the length of his arms. Four large panes of glass surround him on the rostrum. As we crowd around him, looking at his body in its cage of glass, a heady, energetic fuzz swirls around the auditorium. The sound is a high and wavering throb – like I imagine the central nervous system might sound if isolated and amplified – and my body is carried along with it in anxious synchronicity. Athey begins to tend the wig with rough strokes of a paddle brush, and its bristles drag against the crackling blonde acrylic. As the brush catches and pulls, rivulets of blood seep from the artificial hairline. Pulling needles from within its golden thickets, he wrenches the wig from his head, along with a few needles still buried in his scalp. A torrent of blood starts to flow. Athey pulls a sheet of glass against his face and chest, muddling blood, glass, and tattooed skin in pools of light. An arc of blood sprays from a ragged hole in his head and the audience wavers at the scene. Some stand rigid. Others slump under the visual pressure of Athey's performance.

Athey's grisly altarpiece continues with a series of choreographed actions, inundated with blood and hair. In its final moments, a slow torrent of salt falls in a steady shower over Athey's prostrate body. The salt burns and steams, and Athey shivers under its weight, with one hand raised in a panicked gesture – half call, half statement of survival. We can imagine the sting of salt in his wounds, and we breathe the oceanic burn in the air between us. Eventually, he emerges from the chaos of blood, hair, salt, and glass, like a monument to livid, embattled fortitude. He exits the performance space, and the audience that is still standing stays. Our act of looking feels more like a vigil than a scene of spectatorship.

For Gardner, our eyes are 'scorched' by watching Athey's *Self-Obliteration*. The word refers to the effect of the salt cloud that lingered in the air around the glass confines,

but also to the burning of eyes that cry or smart from difficult scenes of looking. The image of an eye traumatised by
its experience of the world takes us back to the sleight of
hand in Buñuel and Dalí's film, where the eye splits open as
though under the pressure of history. In Athey's work, the
audience members leave physically unscathed, bar the few
that faint, retch, or cry. However, in watching his ordeal in
performance, we are asked to identify with the physical and
psychic weight of his experience, as a body under attack, not
least as a survivor of AIDS.

As Buñuel wrote of *Un Chien Andalou*, in a passage cited
by film historian P. Adams Sitney in *Visionary Film* (2000),
'The motivation of the images was [...] purely irrational!
They are as mysterious and inexplicable to the collaborators
as to the spectator. *Nothing*, in the film, *symbolizes anything*'
(p. 4). Similarly, Athey's images refuse the convenient logic
of symbolisation, and cannot be analysed to reveal a single
story or meaning that sets the work free from its affective
difficulty. Instead, the images, sounds, moods, and attendant emotions conspire to produce highly personal responses,
which the audience members work through to come to their
own conclusions about the work.

Beautiful images open onto pleasure or pain, or into
responses that muddle the two affects into conflicted events
of visual experience. By staging the limits of beauty, distil-
ling it into an atrocity exhibition, Athey cites and exceeds the
iconography of Christian martyrdom. His intense imagery
reminds us that bodies are things that tend towards failure –
towards illness, disaster, and death – and by bearing witness

to physical endurance we acknowledge the historicity of the position from which we look. In the visual present, to look at pain in performance is not anachronistic. Neither is it proof of the pathology of an artist who feels pain in performance or torments spectators. Rather, when encouraged to look *with* pain, one remembers more robustly the pains of others, and recalls that the inevitabilities of social interaction include pleasure as well as pain.

In this section, I have explored divergent approaches to reading the production of visual experience in performance. In the earlier examples, I showed that the works of contemporary theatre artists tend towards the invitation to seek pleasure in looking. In the final example, Athey epitomises the attempt to incite pain in the experience of vision. Two accounts of fetishism were introduced to suggest that if the theatre often relies on pleasurable visual experiences, these might be understood as situations where the audience produces meaning through acts of wilful misreading. By reading Annie Sprinkle's work through the psychoanalytic logic of fetishism, we can see that the pleasures of the scene sit in relation to traumatic histories, where a relation between a subject and an object of vision needs to be worked through and reconstituted in order for the theatrical event to produce meaning in a satisfactory way. In Athey's work, the image discloses its traumatic content more readily, because the event is a painful one to behold.

Performance art abounds with powerful images. Attracted to the production of compelling and difficult images in performance, artists often suggest that seeking pleasure or pain in an image can open onto political effects. Interpretive models may be rendered insufficient by performed images, and are therefore refigured and rethought in novel ways. In thinking about how performed images work, we attend to the politics of pleasure, and of pain, and look to the ways in which powerful images mark us as spectators.

Epilogue: the shock of the new

With recent developments in theatre – especially the centrality of un-simulated acts of performance – shocked apprehension is secured as a vital effect of visual experience. Franko B, Annie Sprinkle, and Ron Athey are highly relevant, despite the clear sense in which they set out not to shock but to engage a much broader range of feelings and affects than the theatre is generally primed to produce. As Athey told me in an interview, his work does not issue from 'a strategy of shock, but of generosity. The image or action must be shown. Pulling one's punches may be the tradition [in art and theatre], but I still quiver when live, real-time experience happens' ('Perverse Martyrologies', 2008, p. 507). The emphasis on visibility is important here, and he asserts the political value of showing things that tend otherwise to remain unseen, in theatre, and in popular culture more broadly.

When making visually striking images, performers like Athey might shock their audiences, but they do not rely on this effect as a vehicle for political instrumentality. Nevertheless, I am interested in exploring the visual signs of shock in the body of the spectator. Looking at something that beggars belief can induce a wildly unpredictable set of physiological effects: flinching, laughing, crying, blushing, swooning, fainting, leaving, jeering, booing, and a whole set of other corporeal effects that accompany shock and its siblings. What effects might be produced when an audience is faced with the visual shock of the new?

In the theatre and elsewhere in visual culture, shock is a historically contingent phenomenon. Nineteenth-century mores assumed that breaches in the tightly held codes of decorum were unacceptable, as evidenced, for example, in public and media outcries at the scandalous ending of Henrik Ibsen's *A Doll's House* (Royal Theatre, Copenhagen, 1879). At the close of the play, contemporary viewers saw Nora betray her husband, her family, and her sex for the sake of a wilfully perverse pursuit of education, moral self-determination, and personal freedom. Helmer cries at his fleeing wife, 'I am condemned to humiliation and ruin simply for the weakness of a woman,' and Nora's flight is dramatised by her climactic exit from the stage, the play, and middle-class sociality (pp. 93–94). According to the final stage direction, the visual image of Helmer alone on stage is rounded off by a sonic punch, as 'the street door is slammed shut downstairs' (p. 104). It was decried as the culmination of a nauseating, distasteful work, prompting Ibsen to make reluctant rewrites during the play's early tours.

As this book has sought to show, the contingency of vision is most clearly manifest at the scene of extremity. Put another way, looking looks different when one focuses on that which has not been seen before. The cultural shifts that have taken place across the course of the twentieth century and into the twenty-first have been dependent on the historical contexts from which one has looked at the theatre. Therefore, modernist assaults on vision register differently when re-performed or re-interpreted after the advent of postmodernism. Despite the comparable positions of cultural extremity that various practitioners have inhabited, the progression of cultural experimentation means that the avant-gardist rebellions of the modernists – Beckett or Artaud, for example – are no longer considered to be as outrageous as when contemporary spectators first laid eyes upon them. Likewise, over a century after the fact, Nora's act of self-determination looks increasingly reasonable.

As a value of production and reception, extremity changed irreversibly at a certain point in the twentieth century. The 1960s, specifically, were marked by a disorienting complicity between massive social upheavals and a series of creative disturbances. Extremes of social and cultural progressivity drew their strength from and informed each other. In the US and UK in the 1960s, a range of disenfranchised and marginal subjectivities strived for social and cultural recognition, giving rise to the image of the decade as a moment during which civil rights movements – feminism, black power, lesbian and gay activisms – and anti-capitalist and environmentalist politics conspired to provoke triumphant shifts in popular discourse. Public acts of civil disobedience gave rise to vast social and political upheavals, as well as scholarly innovations and new creative practices.

At the level of cultural practice, specifically, the 1960s saw a relaxing of formal distinctions, and the progressive blurring of divisions between theatre, visual art, film, music, dance, and other categories. The social instabilities produced compensatory responses (including conservative and progressive developments) at the level of scholarship, public reception, and cultural criticism, also ensuring that old distinctions were no longer assured.

My final claim is that these shifts also brought about a new visual experience of shock in the theatre. This new experience was produced by an irresolvable conflict between, on the one hand, the anxious reception of new forms and, on the other hand, the popular belief that the mainstream had suffered such extensive assaults from the experimental fringes that people were now unshockable. The adage that nothing can shock audiences after the reorganisations of the 1960s is one of the most persistent fallacies of cultural reception, even though it is consistently refuted by reactions in tabloid journalism, grievances over public funding of the arts, and popular outcries about the values (or lack thereof) upheld by artistic production.

The belief that nothing we see in art or the theatre can shock us is a decoy for the coincident fact that spectators are promptly offended by feminism, homosexuality, blasphemy, violence, death, prurience, and other images of extremity. When verbal language is squeezed from the practice of theatre, the performed image has an energetic tendency to figure such shocks more profoundly. When we sustain the gap created by the displacement of the text by vision, the effect is unsettling. In such instances, the word may return as a critical instrument to explain away the offences posed by the image. The theatre has shown that the experience of being at a loss for words can be a source of pleasure, as well as of pain.

Throughout this book, I have argued that the ways we look at performed images remind us to ask questions about the meaning of images, but also the meaning of looking. To attend the theatre is to partake in the act of looking, and to see what happens when vision wrestles with a dizzying range of other sensory and conceptual capacities. Moreover, looking is always a historically situated practice, which conceals and reveals a set of social relations. Some of these social relations are pleasing, while others are traumatic. In our visual experience, the act of looking (and looking away) benefits from historical conditions that may remain partially obscured in the tumult of the everyday, but nevertheless cannot be separated from the specificities of the situation from which we look, in theatre no less than in other social realities.

If we look with rigour or naïveté, as voyeurs or cowards, how we are greeted by the stuff of visual experience determines its potential for meaningful acts of reading. The theatre demands that however we see the events that unfold, we must look with care, vigilant to the political possibilities that might emerge from being there, with the performer, and with the work.

further reading

Despite the centrality of looking to the experience of the theatre, relatively little has been published on the visual as a condition of the production of meaning in contemporary theatre and performance studies. The only monograph devoted to the topic is *Visuality in the Theatre: The Locus of Looking* (2008) by Maaike Bleeker, who argues for the contingency of vision as a condition of the ways meaning is produced in theatrical spectatorship. Bleeker's major contribution is to use philosophical theories of vision to track the mid-twentieth-century shift from the avant-garde blurring of art and life to a postmodern, 'deconstructive' critical method.

The disciplines of art history and visual studies have, of course, produced plenty of research on the experience of looking at art, and some of these studies are especially relevant to the study of theatre and performance. Key authors on vision and visuality include John Berger, Jonathan Crary,

Hal Foster, Martin Jay, and W. J. T. Mitchell. Despite the tendency to overlook the specific experiences of vision, theatre and performance studies scholars have written extensively on related themes, including lighting, design, scenography, audiences and reception, and semiotics (see, for example, the work of Elaine Aston, Christopher Baugh, Susan Bennett, Gösta Mauritz Bergman, Frederick Penzel, and Wolfgang Schivelbusch). There is also some interesting work on interdisciplinarity, including specific accounts of relationships between studies in theatre and in visual culture (see the works cited here by Mark Franko and Catherine Soussloff, Shannon Jackson, and Marguerite Tassi).

Visual studies scholars often explore performance art, body art, and/or live art to broaden our understandings of the diversity of artistic practices since the 1960s. The writings of Amelia Jones are paramount in this regard. Nevertheless, theatre has not substantially been seen as relevant to theorisations of visual practice in the twentieth and twenty-first centuries.

Alberti, Leon Battista. *On Painting*. London: Penguin, 1991.

Artaud, Antonin. 'Theatre and the Plague.' *The Theatre and Its Double*. London: John Calder, 1977. 7–22.

Aston, Elaine. *Theatre as Sign-System: A Semiotics of Text and Performance*. London and New York: Routledge, 1991.

Barthes, Roland. *Camera Lucida: Reflections on Photography*. Trans. Richard Howard. New York: Hill & Wang, 1981.

————. 'Rhetoric of the Image.' *Image/Music/Text*. Trans. Stephen Heath. London: Fontana, 1977. 32–51.

Bartlett, Neil. 'Writing Silence.' *Or You Could Kiss Me*. By Bartlett and Handspring Puppet Company. London: Oberon, 2010. 5–10.

Bataille, Georges. 'The Eye.' *Visions of Excess: Selected Writings, 1927–1939*. Trans. Allan Stoekl. Minneapolis: U of Minnesota P, 1985. 17–19.

Baugh, Christopher. *Theatre, Performance and Technology: The Development of Scenography in the Twentieth Century*. Basingstoke: Palgrave Macmillan, 2005.

Beckett, Samuel. 'Breath.' *Complete Dramatic Works*. London: Faber and Faber, 2006. 369–71.

Bennett, Susan. *Theatre Audiences: A Theory of Production and Reception*. London and New York: Routledge, 1990.

Berger, John. *Ways of Seeing*. London: BBC, 1972.

Bergman, Gösta Mauritz. *Lighting in the Theatre*. Lanham: Rowman & Littlefield, 1977.

Bleeker, Maaike. *Visuality in the Theatre: The Locus of Looking*. Basingstoke: Palgrave Macmillan, 2008.

Bourke, Joanna. *Fear: A Cultural History*. London: Virago, 2005.

Bradby, David, and Annie Sparks. *Mise en Scène: French Theatre Now*. London: Methuen, 1997.

Crary, Jonathan. *Techniques of the Observer: On Vision and Modernity in the Nineteenth Century*. Cambridge: MIT Press, 1990.

Crouch, Tim. *The Author*. London: Oberon, 2009.

Davis, Tracy C. ' "Reading Shakespeare by Flashes of Lightning": Challenging the Foundations of Romantic Acting Theory.' *English Literary History* 62.4 (1995): 933–54.

Doyle, Jennifer. 'Critical Tears: Franko B's *I Miss You*.' *Franko B: Blinded by Love*. Ed. Dominic Johnson. Bologna: Damiani, 2006. 41–47.

Etchells, Tim. 'National Review of Live Art Meets a Bloody End.' *Guardian* 25 March 2010. <http://www.guardian.co.uk/stage/2010/mar/24/national-review-of-live-art-ron-athey>.

Foster, Hal. Preface. *Vision and Visuality*. Ed. Foster. Seattle: Bay Press, 1988. ix–xiv.

Foucault, Michel. *The Archaeology of Knowledge*. Trans. Alan Sheridan. London: Routledge, 1989.

Franko, Mark, and Catherine Soussloff. 'Visual and Performance Studies: A New History of Interdisciplinarity.' *Social Text* 73 20.4 (2002): 29–46.

Frazer, James G. *Totemism and Exogamy*. Vol. 1. London: Macmillan, 1910.

Freud, Sigmund. 'Fetishism.' *On Sexuality: Three Essays on the Theory of Sexuality and Other Works*. Trans. James Strachey. London: Penguin, 1977. 351–57.

Gardner, Lyn. 'National Review of Live Art.' *Guardian* 22 March 2010. <http://www.guardian.co.uk/stage/2010/mar/22/national-review-of-live-art>.

Ibsen, Henrik. 'A Doll's House.' *Plays: Two*. Trans. Michael Meyer. London: Methuen, 1980. 22–104.

———. 'Ghosts.' *Ghosts and Other Plays*. Trans. Peter Watts. London: Penguin, 1964. 20–102.

Jackson, Shannon. 'Performing Show and Tell: Disciplines of Visual Culture and Performance.' *Journal of Visual Culture* 4.2 (2005): 163–77.

Jay, Martin. *Downcast Eyes: The Denigration of Vision in Twentieth-Century French Thought*. Berkeley: U of California P, 1993.

———. 'Scopic Regimes of Modernity.' *Vision and Visuality*. Ed. Hal Foster. Seattle: Bay Press, 1988. 3–27.

Jay, Ricky. *Learned Pigs and Fireproof Women*. New York: Farrar, Straus and Giroux, 1986.

Johnson, Dominic. 'Perverse Martyrologies: An Interview with Ron Athey.' *Contemporary Theatre Review* 18.4 (2008): 503–13.

Jones, Amelia. *Body Art / Performing the Subject*. Minneapolis: U of Minnesota P, 1998.

Juno, Andrea. 'Annie Sprinkle.' *Angry Women*. Ed. Andrea Juno and V. Vale. San Francisco: Re/Search Publications, 1991. 23–40.

Marx, Karl. 'The Fetishism of Commodities.' *Selected Writings*. Ed. David McLellan. Oxford: Oxford UP, 1977. 435–43.

McKinney, Joslin, and Philip Butterworth. *The Cambridge Introduction to Scenography*. Cambridge: Cambridge UP, 2009.

Mitchell, W. J. T. *Iconology: Image, Text, Ideology*. Chicago: U of Chicago P, 1987.

———. *What Do Pictures Want? The Lives and Loves of Images*. Chicago: U of Chicago P, 2005.

Myles, Eileen. *Not Me*. New York: Semiotext(e), 1991.

Neilson, Anthony. *Plays: One*. London: Methuen, 1998.

Penzel, Frederick. *Theatre Lighting Before Electricity*. Middleton: Wesleyan UP, 1978.

Rose, Jacqueline. *Sexuality in the Field of Vision*. London: Verso, 1986, 2005.

Rowell, George. *The Victorian Theatre 1792–1914*. Cambridge: Cambridge UP, 1978.

Schivelbusch, Wolfgang. *Disenchanted Night: The Industrialisation of Light in the Nineteenth Century*. Berkeley: U of California P, 1995.

Schneider, Rebecca. 'On Taking the Blind in Hand.' *Contemporary Theatre Review* 10.3 (2000): 23–38.

————. *The Explicit Body in Performance*. London: Routledge, 1997.

Sitney, P. Adams. *Visionary Film: The American Avant-Garde, 1943–2000*. Oxford: Oxford UP, 2000.

Steiner, Wendy. *The Scandal of Pleasure: Art in an Age of Fundamentalism*. Chicago: U of Chicago P, 1995.

Tassi, Marguerite A. *The Scandal of Images: Iconoclasm, Eroticism, and Painting in Early Modern Drama*. Selingsgrove: Susquehanna UP, 2005.

Williams, Linda. *Hard Core: Power, Pleasure, and the 'Frenzy of the Visible.'* Berkeley: U of California P, 1999.

Williams, Tennessee. *Cat on a Hot Tin Roof*. London: Methuen Drama, 2010.

index